HAUGHEY
PRINCE OF POWER

CONOR LENIHAN

BLACKWATER PRESS

ISBN 978-1-909974-06-7

© Conor Lenihan, 2015

Cover Image: RTÉ Stills Library

BWP Ltd., 1-5 North Frederick Street, Dublin 1

Printed in the Republic of Ireland.

jloconnor@eircom.net

Preface

The decision to write this book arose from a conversation in my mother's kitchen during the early part of 2015 between the publisher John O'Connor and myself. For years I had in my mind to do a book on Haughey. In fact, I even discussed this possibility with Charlie Haughey himself on a visit to him in his home, Abbeville. However, I was serving in government at that point and the timing was wrong.

When John suggested that now was the time to work on it, I immediately jumped at the chance. My father, the late Brian Lenihan Senior, was once famously described, by Haughey, as his 'friend of 30 years'. The irony of course is that Haughey made this comment while denying that he was going to ask my father for his resignation, in the course of the Presidential election of 1990. That very day he had urged my father to resign. Within a day, frightened by his coalition partners, Haughey sacked my father.

I am loathe to describe this book as a biography as it mixes between straight biographical material and reminiscences of my own, as well as the views of my father as conveyed to me by him. I am very grateful to those writers who have already written about Haughey and many of them are quoted throughout the book. For the 1960s I am thankful to two Lemass biographers, John Horgan, and Bryce Evans. In relation to specific biographies of Haughey I have quoted from books by T. Ryle Dwyer and Bruce Arnold. In addition to this I have drawn from Patrick Maume's Monograph for the Royal Irish Academy that subsequently became the Haughey entry in the Dictionary of Irish Biography.

Haughey was a deeply polarising figure in Irish politics. It was hard to be neutral about him. The level and extent of his corruption, and acceptance of money from businessmen only emerged after he retired. The pictures painted by the McCracken and Moriarty tribunals are not pretty. In this book I have tried to incorporate the different and competing depictions of him from varied sources.

Hopefully a younger generation will get a glimpse from this book of what it was like to live through the Haughey era. Times have moved on and hopefully Ireland will be a better place.

I would emphasise that Haughey was atypical amongst politicians in Ireland. In defence of my former profession I would say that well over 90% of those elected to Dáil Éireann, over the years, are idealistic and well-motivated people. In my experience of 14 years in Leinster House, Irish politicians work extremely hard for very little actual reward.

The Haughey experience, in this sense, is tragic as it has brought the profession of politics through the mud. Hopefully a younger generation will gravitate towards politics with the intellectual capacity of Haughey but not with his terrible flaws about money.

I wish to thank my publisher John O'Connor, the editorial team at Blackwater Press and my extended family and friends who offered great advice while I was writing this book.

In particular I would like to thank my mother Ann and sister Anita for their helpful support. I would also like to thank a friend from London, Bill Gingles, who was not only encouraging but read drafts and suggested some real improvements. Paddy Kilmartin, a good friend, was also generous with his advice. My cousin Padraig Lenihan, a professional historian, also gave me valuable insight before I started to write this book.

I would like to thank my wife Nikita for her support, without which, this book could not have been written. My children Brian, Jack, Alex, Aoife and Patrick Joseph are a real source of inspiration as are the mothers that truly rear them.

Conor Lenihan
November 2015

Contents

CHAPTER ONE
TRIBUNAL

It is not often that one hears a claim to the effect that an adult life has been heavily influenced by the dominant presence of an historical figure. But mine was. And in my case that figure was one Charles J. Haughey.

I was born in 1963 and growing up in a political household I learnt of Mr Haughey by osmosis, casual eavesdropping on my parents' conversations with friends and the gossip he Haughey seemed to generate. Even in the late 1960s he was a major subject of conversation. When the mothers gathered in our kitchen for their mid-morning tea, Haughey was often up for discussion. Naturally, opinions varied with Haughey's reputational stock rising and falling within a single trading session. He was regarded with a curious mixture of envy, resentment and outright awe. He tended to divide people even then. He was a player and it had all to do with all of the things that Catholic Ireland was not meant to talk about – money, sex and power.

In a country that had at the time become used to poverty, emigration and a culture of concealed or genteel affluence, Haughey stood out. He had money, an abundance of it, he rode to hounds and in addition to that he had married well. An up-and-coming accountant, he had married the daughter of the most influential man in the state – the country's *primus inter pares*, the Taoiseach or Prime Minister, Seán Lemass. Lemass was not just any old Minister who reached the top, he was revered for his focus on domestic industry, his opening of the country to outside investment and as a moderniser. Lemass, in a real sense, was the architect of modern Ireland with all its flaws and benefits. A man ahead of his time.

Haughey's life up to the 1960s reads like a Walt Disney cartoon classic with him playing the humble commoner who marries the Princess. From an ordinary background, he married into a family of serious power. In short order he would become an elected member of the Dáil, sell his Raheny home for a small fortune and move into a Gandon mansion in North County Dublin. By any contemporary yardstick this was success on a grand scale. A young man with all this success could well be prone to an excess of confidence. His critics suggested a malevolent arrogance. One thing was certain – he could not be ignored.

He evoked strong, often visceral sentiment. His staunchest media critic, the columnist and writer Bruce Arnold, sums up Haughey in his biography *Haughey: His Life and Unlucky Deeds:*

> *"He is a man of immense charm with a compelling physical presence, despite his smallness of stature. This has caused many to liken him to Napoleon. He moves with economy of gesture and energy. His well-tailored suits conceal a plumpness not unlike the French emperor. His handshake is without warmth or commitment; a soft, limp paddle of flesh is offered disdainfully and received humbly. Into his eyes are concentrated all his feelings and they are essentially cold and suspicious; the stare is reptilian."*

From the 1960s onwards Haughey was acquiring both a legend and enemies. In legend terms he was a sometime 1920s style mogul, a de Medici Renaissance prince and, according to some local scribes, a Gaelic tribal chief. The metaphors used to describe him could be variously intensely flattering, wounding and extreme. The prosaic reality was that he was one of the first Irish politicians to hire a professional publicist. The gals around my Mum's kitchen table expressed skepticism about the matinee idol, touched up photos that his handlers pushed on the press. But despite the skepticism about his good looks, there was always one of the mums who admitted that she found him handsome.

His political impact in the 1960s was brash. Before he came on the scene, a certain self-abnegation and modest living was not just expected, but the order of the day when it came to politics. The old revolutionaries were not icons of fashion, nor fans of conspicuous consumption, but rather political men in long dark coats, sometimes wearing sombre hats. Conversely, Haughey was occasionally photographed in that most upper crust English affectation, the top hat.

In addition to commentary on his lavish lifestyle, the source of his fortune, as early as the 1960s, was also becoming a source of both controversy and comment. T. Ryle Dwyer, a more sympathetic biographer, writes in *Charlie*:

> *"He quickly amassed a considerable fortune at a time when politics was not a particularly well paid profession. In 1960 he bought Grangemore, a large Victorian mansion on a 15-acre site in Raheny in north Dublin. He reportedly paid around £50,000 and sold it before the end of the decade for over four times that amount after planning permission had been granted to build houses on the land. In the meantime he managed to buy a farm in Ashbourne, Co Meath, purchased a chicken hatchery, some race horses, and bought Innishvicillaun – one of the Blasket Islands, some ten miles off the coast of Kerry."*

The sale of his Raheny home became the first significant controversy in his career. The *Evening Herald*, according to Ryle Dwyer, ran a sensational report claiming that the

Raheny property had been purchased by Mr Haughey's developer friend, Matt Gallagher, for over £200,000. The combination of the money involved and development potential of the site made it a combustible controversy with rivals in Fine Gael and the Labour party raising it in both the Dáil and on the doorsteps in his constituency. Conor Cruise O'Brien, his Labour Party rival in the constituency, raised it in the constituency campaign for the 1969 general election. O'Brien was to become a lifelong critic of Haughey and in this campaign pointed to the "Fianna Fáil speculator-orientated oligarchy."[1] If O'Brien was to become a persistent critic, the Gallaghers (Matt and son Patrick), who purchased the house, were to become lifelong financial backers.

The Moriarty Tribunal, established in 1997, was tasked to investigate the source of payments to Haughey and would feature Patrick Gallagher's contributions to the loan write-off deal, arranged by AIB Bank, in 1979. That loan was for over a million pounds and heavily discounted by the bank. The significance is that this loan was squared off subsequent to Haughey's ascent to the office of Taoiseach. The acute irony of course is that just at the point when Haughey was enjoying his greatest success in politics he was in fact heavily indebted to the banks or, more bluntly, utterly broke. It seems that the banks at this stage were running in fear of upsetting the country's newly ensconced leader and more than willing to facilitate a resolution of the Haughey indebtedness. According to an obituary piece on Haughey in the *Economist* magazine, the £400,000 had been written off the loan after Haughey had warned the bank, "I can be a very troublesome adversary". In 1979 at least one newspaper published an article claiming that Haughey owed a million pound sum to the bank. The story was rebutted, trenchantly, in a press release from AIB. The key point is that while rumours abounded about both

[1]Dwyer, T. Ryle *Charlie*, Gill & Macmillan (1987), p. 69

his wealth and indebtedness, hard information by way of proof was hard to come by. A few diehard insiders might have known the facts but the wider public was in the dark. Within Fianna Fáil and the wider country, the wilder the rumours that were circulated about Haughey, irrespective of whether based on fact or fantasy, the more likely they were to polarize people into opposite camps. Supporters became more ardent – pleading dirty tricks by the opposition – and the opponents more desperate in their approach to removing him from power.

Haughey's early efforts in politics were not indicative of someone who enjoyed great popularity. It took him several outings before he was eventually successful, notwithstanding the resources he had at his disposal and the connection he enjoyed through marriage. My father, the late Brian Lenihan Senior, always made the point that while Haughey had huge executive skills and intellect he was not by any means a 'natural politician'. In other words, the people pleasing skills were for the most part absent. He was awkward and reserved in that respect. The Lemass biographer Bryce Evans makes the point:

> *"Haughey's early political career was disappointing. He ran unsuccessfully for the Dáil in Dublin North East in 1951 and 1954. He was co-opted onto Dublin Corporation in 1953 but suffered the ignominy of losing his seat the local elections in 1955."*[2]

Haughey was eventually elected to the Dáil in 1957. His first big break in politics came in May of 1960 when his father-in-law and then-Taoiseach Seán Lemass offered him a position in the government as a Parliamentary Secretary to the Minister for Justice Oscar Traynor. Lemass, according to Haughey, told him: "As Taoiseach it is my duty to offer you the post of Parliamentary Secretary and as your father-in-

---

[2]Evans, Bryce, *Seán Lemass, Democratic Dictator*, The Collins Press, 2011, p. 198

law I am advising you not to take it."[3] It seems Seán Lemass might have been happier for the security and prosperity of his daughter and son-in-law in the long run if Haughey had stayed on the backbenches while continuing to earn money from his accountancy practice. From a very early point in his climb up the political ladder, Haughey had become highly dependent on money as a guarantor of political success. In brief, he had evolved a high-maintenance lifestyle both in his personal life and his political career.

Much of his appeal depended on the notion that he himself was a wealthy, ambitious man who could also bring wealth and success to the country itself. In a way, he was seen in this opening phase of his career to be a man with a sort of Midas touch and tremendous business acumen. Prior to his death, I spoke to Patrick Gallagher about the Haughey mystique. He claimed to me and also in an interview with the *Sunday Business Post* that he and other successful businessmen had supported Haughey in his lifestyle out of a belief that Ireland, as a post-colonial country, required an icon of sorts. Haughey, he said, was put both metaphorically and physically in the saddle of the horse in order that he could live this life, that in a previous era, could only be enjoyed by the Anglo-Irish aristocracy of old. Gallagher and others felt that the only way Ireland could be truly independent and confident was if the people could see that the native Irish were now clearly in charge. It was a somewhat preposterous boast on Gallagher's part, but a belief I myself witnessed as a regular feature amongst those who gave money to Haughey. Over the years, in particular since the Tribunal, I have come across many individual businesspeople who have confessed with great pride and humour the enjoyment they got from visits to Haughey's Kinsealy home. It seems that contributing to Haughey's lifestyle, for some at least, was confirmatory of their insider

---

[3]Arnold, Bruce, *Haughey – His life and Unlucky Deeds*, Harper Collins, 1993, p. 29

status. Haughey also seemed to have an elaborate ritual when it came to keeping people on tenterhooks in relation to what they might be seeking in return. There was a touch of the Mafia Don about the whole act, a Mafia Don without of course the sordid violence. Haughey's act was grist to the mill for caricaturists. Even the media themselves, became enthralled to the point where many moaned about the tiresome boredom of the new, squeaky clean, politics that was being served up in place of Haughey in the wake of his retirement in 1992. The irony is of course that the country was in a bleak space when Haughey was in office in the 1980s. But political activism was something of a passionate pursuit in this period, despite the high unemployment and emigration. As I remember it there were rowdy party meetings, long speeches and a very active internal debate within Fianna Fáil and that was just at foot-soldier level.

At the parliamentary level the drama was just as compelling. The endless conflicts over Haughey, the claims and counter-claims, and in particular the vicious infighting which could involve factions, rival personalities and even disputes over policy. The competing views were very evident and some activists who were married fell out because their loved ones went with the other side. The scene got even more interesting when one factored in not just the Haughey-O'Malley dispute but the grander clash of intellects between ruthless, aggrandising Haughey, and the fabled Garret 'The Good' FitzGerald. Constituency meetings, held on a monthly basis, were often attended by more than a hundred and twenty party members. There was real heat in the room. The sitting TDs were not the subjects of adulation but more often robust criticism. Within the Ógra, or youth wing of the party, there was also this fevered struggle between those seen as loyal to the leadership of Haughey and those who were either overtly or covertly entertaining doubts. Haughey's perceived strength on the 'National Question' locked-in a great deal of support within the party but also with the wider public. FitzGerald's vision of a more conciliatory approach to both Unionists and London was seen to be utter anathema to those who considered themselves republican. In this sense, Haughey was able to present himself as being a talisman for a more radical nationalism in the republican tradition.

Sacked by Jack Lynch and subsequently brought before the courts, his treatment at the time of the 1970 Arms Trial, over a plan to import weapons for the IRA in the North of Ireland, had won him a lot of sympathy. The Arms controversy was pivotal in terms of shaping views of him and determining his subsequent journey up the political ladder. In short it gave Haughey the 'whiff of cordite' and underlined both the radicalism and danger he presented to the established order. Rumours of meetings between him and the Army Council of the IRA pursued him throughout his career afterwards. This made him a connected person in a way that many might have both respected and feared.

In the 1980s Haughey's opportunism in championing conservatism on social issues like contraception, divorce and abortion tended to alienate some of the more liberal members of society, again by polarizing the debate, the corollary was that he locked in the loyal support of lay Catholics who otherwise might have had an utter disdain for his lifestyle. The pro-life constituency was given free rein over party policy on these matters to a point where it was becoming unhealthy and at odds with the strictly personal and more liberal choices being made by the wider electorate. With these types of contradiction within the party, many became cynical and a grouping around the opponents of Haughey began to either drift away or find themselves a new political party. The internal dissidents were defeated, with some of them peeling off to form the Progressive Democrats. Dissidents who stayed, like Joe Walsh and Séamus Brennan, thrived and achieved cabinet rank under either Haughey or subsequent leaders. Des Hanafin, the chief party fundraiser under Haughey's predecessor Jack Lynch, underwent a remarkable transformation. He found, when Haughey took over the party, that he was pushed out of the equation as the new leader wrested the fundraising machinery under his own personal control. Later, Hanafin was to re-emerge in Haughey's affections due to the fact that Hanafin was now a leading lay champion of the pro-life cause. Knighted by the Pope, Des Hanafin successfully persuaded Haughey to adopt the cause, and over the years to follow, anti-abortion activists became an integrated part of the Haughey personal machine providing much-needed defence for him against both internal and external critics.

The only interesting point about Haughey's positioning in relation to the pro-life issue was how tactical the whole thing was. Prior to taking the decision to opt for the God squad he had taken a great deal of soundings on the issue. For instance, my father was asked to meet with the lobby group representing those who wanted to see divorce introduced to Ireland. As it happened, the main figure at the time was a man called John O'Connor, who ran a successful engineering business, and was father to the singer Sinéad O'Connor. His son Joe, subsequently a writer, was in UCD with me and was also a member of the Labour party. He and I had a lot of friends in common. My father made contact with the Divorce Action Group. By nature and instinct my father was a progressive or small 'L' liberal. He wanted to see society modernised and viewed the whole Catholic nature of the state as being at odds with its republican ethos. The decision to meet with the Divorce Action Group was also significant because at this point in his career under Haughey, my father had overall responsibility for party policy and its development. His outreach to O'Connor seemed to have gone well and my father was enthusiastic about the possibility of Fianna Fáil, if not actually campaigning for divorce, allowing its party supporters a 'free vote' on the issue. He wanted a situation whereby people, like himself, could advocate a 'Yes' vote with others stating the opposite. He seemed to be buoyed up by the idea that he would get this past Haughey. He said as much to O'Connor in my hearing when he met with him in the Dáil.

The idea that Fianna Fáil would position itself as not being hostile to measures like divorce seemed very positive to my younger mind. John O'Connor would have been happy with Fianna Fáil being neutral and would have viewed it as a bonus if individual, and prominent, members were publicly advocating a yes to divorce. As things turned out, Haughey was not inclined to see things the same way as my father did. Haughey viewed the role of an opposition party as simply to oppose the government on all and every occasion. The opportunity to give Garret FitzGerald a further knock over the divorce issue was too great an opportunity for him to ignore. Garret FitzGerald had positioned himself as a champion of a more 'pluralist Ireland' and had reaped a significant dividend from younger, more liberal, voters as a result.

As the writer John Waters puts it:

"FitzGerald had been an almost unmitigated failure as a politician. By the end of the 1982-87 Fine Gael/ Labour coalition, the dream had begun to unravel and the sheen was wearing off FitzGerald's liberal halo. The expectations he had engendered with his rhetoric about a constitutional crusade against sectarianism and conservatism had foundered on the rocks of hard political reality. Many who has risen to his call were disillusioned by what was perceived to be his backtracking on abortion and his dissembling on other issues."[4]

---

[4]Waters, John, *Was it for This? Why Ireland lost the Plot*, Transworld Publishers, 2012

Given the extent of the FitzGerald failure both in terms of his personal crusade and his determination to put 'financial rectitude' into the public finances, the way was paved for Charles Haughey to return to power. When Haughey did return to power in 1987 it was again the case that he would do so without having the full mandate of an absolute Dáil majority. Yet, despite the absence of a majority, it was to be his most successful period in office. The actual result in the 1987 general election was a severe disappointment to him. In the days after the election my father described him to be in a very depressed state, even more so, than was the case in his many years in the wilderness following the setback he received due to the Arms Trial in 1970. The Haughey critics, inside and outside the party, had always made much of the fact that he had failed consistently to win a Dáil majority. He was not the first Taoiseach or Fianna Fáil leader to rule without a majority but the criticism clearly stung him. The fact that he had never won a majority could easily be contrasted with the enormous electoral success of his predecessor Jack Lynch. The absence of a majority under his leadership was also a way for his opponents to take from his legitimacy. However, his enormous personal appeal had been consistently reaffirmed in all of the elections in his Dublin constituency from 1957 onwards.

The question of Haughey's political legitimacy was to be a constant feature throughout his career. It had begun in the 1960s with rumours about his money-making exploits. When he became Taoiseach in 1979 this question mark over his persona and personal ambition was formalised when the then leader of the opposition Garret FitzGerald made his controversial 'flawed pedigree' speech in response to Haughey's nomination for the position of Taoiseach.

Apart from the controversy in relation to the Arms Trial there was no doubt that the FitzGerald speech, while mainly political, was also taking in, *inter alia*, a strong insinuation about the source of Haughey's enormous wealth and lifestyle. The money and lifestyle issues were of course never explicitly mentioned by FitzGerald but he spoke about the issue of 'motive' enough to allow the reader or listener to the speech make up his or her own mind without having to dig further:

> *"Deputy Haughey presents himself here, seeking to be invested in office as the seventh in this line, but he comes with a flawed pedigree. His motives can be judged ultimately only by God but we cannot ignore the fact that he differs from his predecessors in that these motives have been and are widely impugned, most notably but by no means exclusively, by people within his own Party, people close to him who have observed his actions for many years and who have made their human, interim judgment on him. They and others, both in and out of public life, have attributed to him an overwhelming ambition which they do not see as a simple emanation of a desire to serve but rather as a wish to dominate, even to own the State."*

Haughey's return to power in 1987 was remarkable at a number of levels. He had managed to disappoint his most ardent of supporters by identifying the problems in the public finances only to abandon solving them. His arrival in power in 1979 had coincided with the arrival of Mrs Thatcher across the water in Britain. Both were seen as hard-headed exponents of economic efficiency. Thatcher more than matched up to her image on the economy while Haughey flattered to deceive. Since that failure over the public finances he had been the subject of robust attack from within his own party as well as from an opposition led by Garret FitzGerald which came very close to toppling Fianna Fáil's easy dominance of the political system. In 1987 Haughey set out to restore the public finances and ameliorate relations with Britain, the source of much suspicion due to his own provocative stance on the invasion of the Falkland Islands by Mrs Thatcher. While the governments he led after 1987 were amongst the most successful he ran he was only to be given a further four years in public office.

Less than five years after his retirement his peace was to be again disturbed by revelations of lavish financial donations given to him by prominent members of the business community. His last years of life were to be dominated by his own finances as opposed to the public finances. It began as rumours about a one million pound donation from a prominent businessman. In quick speed the media began reporting about a 'Mr You Know Who' in relation to these controversial payments. It got to the point where most people, or the proverbial dogs in the street, were barking Haughey's name. Eventually the dam, holding back the torrent of rumours, was burst and it was revealed publicly that Haughey had received a one million pound payment from the supermarket boss Ben Dunne. The news of the payment had only in fact emerged because of an internal row within the Dunnes Stores Group as Ben saw control over the Group wrested from his grip by his formidable and ultimately victorious sister Margaret Heffernan. Two icons of Irish life were soon to crash to the ground. Ben Dunne had become a hugely well-known personality thanks to his 'Better Value beats Them All' slogan with regard to the bargains to be had in his stores. Another politician, Michael Lowry, of Fine Gael was also caught up in the backlash over the dispute within the Dunne family. The embarrassment for the State was considerable in relation to Haughey, given his status as a former Taoiseach and ruler of the country. Initially the government, led by John Bruton, tasked a retired Judge, Mr Justice Buchanan to look into the issues. This was followed by a more formal inquiry by Mr Justice McCracken. McCracken reported back swiftly and gave evidence of secretive payments to

Haughey from Dunne as well as, a well planned, series of offshore payments to Haughey through accounts held with Ansbacher Bank, leading to a trail of money through Guinness Mahon Bank to the offshore location of the Cayman islands in the Caribbean. The Ansbacher accounts were a series of numbered and anonymous accounts which enabled the deposit holders to have their money held offshore but controlled from an office in Dublin. In effect, the accounts were run by a secretary and the accountant Des Traynor who had been for a long time the personal accountant to Haughey. The revelation of such elaborate measures to hide the money trail to Haughey caused a great deal of public anger.

Bertie Ahern, as leader of Fianna Fáil in opposition, became forthright in demanding a fuller investigation into the money trail to both Haughey and Lowry. Behind the scenes, I was helping Ahern in his bid to become Taoiseach. Even without the revelations about Haughey's money, Ahern was already being depicted as having an umbilical cord of connection to Haughey and his wing of the Fianna Fáil party. The fact that Ahern's career had thrived under Haughey did not help. The clearly admiring quotation once given by Haughey about Bertie Ahern had stuck in a lot of ears: "The most ruthless, the most cunning, the most devious of them all". I and others connected to Ahern were urging him to create 'clear blue water' between himself and the Haughey past. For all of these reasons Ahern was not behind the door when it came to calls for a fuller investigation of Haughey. His vehemence in demanding action from the Bruton government culminated in an Ard Fhéis speech where he stated he would establish his own Tribunal of Inquiry into the matter when he formed a government. Suspicions about Ahern abated while those about Haughey increased. Ahern won the 1997 general election and proceeded to create another Tribunal of Inquiry into Haughey. This one was to be headed up by Mr

Justice Moriarty. It had a wider and more extensive remit and would take over ten years to finish its inquiries with a final report on the allegations levelled at both Haughey and Lowry. In the meantime Mary Harney, as leader of the Progressive Democrats, had formed a coalition government with Fianna Fáil. As a long time opponent of Haughey both within and outside Fianna Fáil, she too would have been keen that Haughey was fully investigated. Her party had been founded as a direct result of her and others failure to topple Haughey as leader of Fianna Fáil. Frustrations over Haughey's position on the public finances, taxation and the North of Ireland were the key elements in the formation of the Progressive Democrats.

The McCracken report had been praised with the speed with which it deliberated and uncovered the important issues. Apart from the series of offshore accounts and under the counter payments made to Haughey, the McCracken Tribunal also found evidence that Haughey had in effect tried to obstruct the work of the Tribunal. The Director of Public Prosecutions sent forward a prosecution case. However, in the days and weeks before the case came up in court the Tánaiste Mary Harney gave an interview to a Sunday newspaper. It was one of those broad-ranging public interviews that politicians give from time to time. It filled the front page of the supplement in the newspaper. In the middle of the interview she expressed the hope that Haughey would be convicted in the courts and effectively serve a jail sentence. The comments appeared innocuous and not even the mainstay of the article itself. Even the legally untutored eye could tell the interview was a considerable hostage to fortune. It created a ready-made defence for Haughey's lawyers that he could not receive a fair trial because of prejudicial media coverage and commentary. His court lawyers could argue not only of prejudice on the part of the media but also with regards to the government itself through the constitutional position of Tánaiste.

Judge Kevin Haugh of the Circuit Court, on hearing the case in relation to Haughey, decided to postpone 'indefinitely' a trial due to what he termed a 'real and substantial risk' that the former Taoiseach would not be able to get a fair trial. His decision was upheld by the High Court with the higher court stating that it was open to the Director of Public Prosecutions to re-enter a case. In the event this did not happen. Once again, according to the lore, Charles Haughey had been lucky. It was often repeated during his long career that he had been 'cursed by his friends and blessed with his enemies'. Mary Harney, clearly an enemy, had now provided the quotes that helped the Judge to conclude that Haughey could not receive a fair trial. The Judge cited the Harney comments and a handbill in circulation for a public meeting entitled 'jail the corrupt politicians' that was being run by one of the country's socialist fringe parties, as evidence that Mr Haughey could not receive a fair trial. Mary Harney was not flavour of the month and many, including myself, now a Dáil deputy found it a profoundly ironic twist of fate. Mary Harney, a college-debating figure, had come to prominence as a young appointee to the Senate by Jack Lynch. However her real claim to fame in the early part of her career was her steadfast opposition to Charles Haughey.

Despite this failure to jail Haughey in relation to obstruction of a public tribunal, another tribunal would soon be underway. The Moriarty Tribunal suited many. Fianna Fáil under Bertie Ahern could be seen to be investigating its past, without fear or favour. It also involved the investigation of a rival Fine Gael cabinet minister thus spreading the potential blame that could be heaped on Fianna Fáil. The Moriarty Tribunal also reassured the Progressive Democrats that they had formed a government with what was, in effect, a new Fianna Fáil far removed from its past under Haughey. The Dáil in its wisdom or lack of wisdom had set no end date for the conclusion of the Tribunal and its investigations. Any effort to speed up or curtail the inquiry in its investigations would have led to allegations of political interference and in particular to those now in office, namely Fianna Fáil and the Progressive Democrats. The fact that Fine Gael was also the subject of potential embarrassment made it difficult to wind down this Tribunal, no matter what the cost to the taxpayer. That said, the Moriarty Tribunal report uncovered payments in excess of €11.6 million to Haughey over a 17-year period. The Tribunal, by its own formulation, stated that the amount received by Haughey was equivalent to €45 million at the time of the publication of the report. By any yardstick this was a lot of money. It came as a shock to many who had supported Haughey down the years. Few if anybody had quite realised that he had been substantially broke and dependent on donors for quite such a long time.

CHAPTER TWO

EARLY YEARS

Charles Haughey was born in 1925, which made him five years older than my father, the late Brian Lenihan Senior. From what my own family have told me, they did not meet until they had both graduated into the political scene in Ireland. Their times at University College Dublin and at the King's Inns did not coincide. That neither man had met the other before being active in politics is hardly a surprise. My father grew up in the midlands town of Athlone, County Westmeath while Haughey was raised, predominantly, in Donnycarney on Dublin's north side. One was a country boy, the other immersed in the city. Despite the differences in where they were brought up they had a lot in common. Both were sons of men who had served in the IRA and who had subsequently, under the influence of Michael Collins, become commissioned officers in the Free State Army. Both my father and Charles Haughey, despite the fact that their fathers were pro-treaty, ended up working for Fianna Fáil, the party that had emerged from that bitterest of conflicts, the Irish Civil War. The forefathers of the party had been on the anti-treaty side while the Lenihan and Haughey parents had been defending that treaty against armed insurrection and attack. They were "Free Staters", a term of abuse in those circles that went on to form Fianna

Fáil from the ashes of defeat in the civil war. There was a shared, or further, coincidence in the background of both my grandfather and the father of Charles Haughey. As members of the IRA, they had both been given tasks that General Collins had devised to undermine the newly-created Unionist statelet that had come into being because of the Anglo-Irish Treaty signed with the British. My own grandfather was part of a unit, set up by Collins, that was to prepare for an invasion of the North. Charles Haughey's father Seán was a leading member of the IRA in County Derry where he and his wife Sarah were from. When Charles Haughey became Taoiseach for the first time in 1979 the Reverend Ian Paisley described him as 'the son of a gun-runner from Swatragh'. The Reverend Paisley was correct, if not sharing the Haughey family pride in that fact.

Charles Haughey was born in Castlebar in County Mayo, where his father was then serving as an army officer. Little has been told of the exact circumstances of his birth. A relation of Colonel Clancy, a legendary veteran of the Free State Army, once told me that Clancy had been in the house in Mayo the day that Charlie was born. Apparently he, Seán Haughey and other men were downstairs, playing cards, while the women upstairs assisted at the birth. I remember telling Charlie of the story regaled to me by the Clancy relation. He laughed a little at the story, confirming the family friendship with Clancy, but most of all at the idea that a father would do anything of the like in the modern age, mentioning that all of his sons attended at their children's births. Haughey biographer Bruce Arnold takes up the story of his father's involvement in the IRA:

"The Haugheys did not come from Mayo, however, but from County Derry, where Seán had been active in the War of Independence. In January 1919 he was second-in-command of a South Derry battalion of Irish Volunteers. In 1922 he was in command of a brigade."[5]

[5]Arnold, Bruce, *Haughey – His Life and Unlucky Deeds*, Harper Collins, 1993, p. 9

The legacy of that civil war division of the country in their parents' generation made both my own father, and to a certain extent Haughey, obsessive about notions of party and national unity. They felt, perhaps more than many others, that a sense of discipline, purpose and unity were important features of political success. They clung to an earlier era in terms of discipline, a military definition in fact, which characterised the generation that had helped achieve Irish independence for the 26 counties. Prior to the changes in the Fianna Fáil organisation, brought about by Seán Lemass in the 1950s, the Party was essentially run by a tight-knit group of revolutionary era, dyed-in-the-wool, IRA men who had seen through difficult times together. It was not unusual for suspicion to be thrown in the direction of both my father and Haughey because their fathers had been on the opposite side during the civil war. My father frequently brought me to functions, rallies and sporting events from a very young age. At various events over the years one would come into contact with some of these survivors of the War of Independence or Civil War. These men or women were made of a much tougher weave than those who began to succeed their generation as the 1940s gave way to the 50s and 60s. This was brought home to me when I would attend commemorative events like the annual 1916 commemoration at Arbour Hill. They were austere, or unflashy, by dress style. The men wore dark suits, complete with ties, sometimes stiff collars, and the women tweed or dark fabric dresses complete with brooches pinned to their jacket collars, hats or coats. If they were surviving widows of those that had died in the national struggle they would often wear the medals their loved ones had won. They were all fairly taciturn and rarely spoke about their role in the struggle. Sometimes my father would go back to a local hotel, located near the Phoenix Park gates, to mix with them and other party activists after the commemoration. There was a strict division between those ordinary members of the party and those that had actually served. There was an inner room, set aside, for those that had fought. It would be full of smoke from the cigarettes and pipes being consumed. They would grab a word in my father's ear as he moved along. They would frequently make hushed references to 'the Chief' the general term of reverence extended to de Valera. I never once heard him referred to by name at these gatherings. He was a figure commanding great respect and while alive the pervading spirit of the party. Amid the smoke, very occasionally, a song would reach up from the lips of a veteran. The one that seemed to resonate most was 'A Nation Once Again', a kind of unofficial anthem, in those traditional republican circles. Growing up, as I did in the 1960s, in such close proximity to those that had fought to set up the state, made you very conscious of the earlier generation and to an extent proud of the achievements of the new Irish State.

If my own feelings were nationalist as I grew up in the 1960s, one can only imagine the strong feelings that must have been present in the Haughey home in Donnycarney. Here was a family from Derry, directly impacted by the events surrounding the birth of the new state and in a real sense cut off from relatives on the other side of the border imposed by the Treaty. In a television documentary entitled *'My Ireland'* made years later in the 1980s while Haughey was in opposition, Haughey faced the camera alongside a British army border checkpoint, and intoned in his gravelly voice of the feelings of 'anger and resentment' that welled up in him when he passed these living reminders of the partition imposed on Ireland. It was easy for some to be cynical about such a broadcast but a more long-sighted view would understand precisely why Haughey would chose to include this, given his own family background in Derry. It was also a reminder to a largely British viewing audience that the problems of Northern Ireland could not be simply and continually ignored. As Bruce Arnold points out in his biography of Haughey, many of his summers were in spent in Swatragh in County Derry:

> *"There were still members of the family in Swatragh and Charles also spent periods there living with his*

grandmother, at times going to the local school at Corlecky. In 1933 the family settled in Donnycarney and it was from there that he went to the Christian Brothers' primary school, Scoil Iosef, in Marino."[6]

A friend of Haughey's from his primary school days, Emmet Memery, describes him as being very popular in school: "He was a very good scholar. It was as plain as a button. He won scholarships. Scoil Mhuire Marino won all the cups when Haughey was there. He was a great hurler and footballer too. Way ahead of the rest."[7]

The young Charles Haughey appeared to be a remarkable student and proceeded to win two separate scholarships, one to go to University College Dublin, through a National University Scholarship, and a second while still in school given by Dublin Corporation. My mother, years later when tearing up some floorboards in our house, came across an old edition of the *Irish Press* where the young Haughey was interviewed by the newspaper about his winning of the Corporation Scholarship. In it he touchingly stated that he wanted to do well in order to look after his mother. Haughey was also good at sport, playing both hurling and Gaelic football for those stalwart clubs of Dublin's north side namely St Vincent's and Parnell's. He won a Dublin Senior Football Championship medal with Parnell's in 1945. His brother Jock played on the full Dublin County side. The extensive contacts made within the GAA were to serve him well when he went about building up his own accountancy firm. It must also have been of invaluable assistance as he made his made his way up the political ladder. Given the influence his father had on him, he also joined the local, or volunteer defence forces, which subsequently became known as the FCA. He achieved the officer rank of Lieutenant. A friend and constituent of mine from the Tallaght area

---

[6] Arnold, Bruce, *Haughey – His Life and Unlucky Deeds*, Harper Collins, 1993, p. 12

[7] Emmet Memery, former Chairman of St Vincent's GAA Club, in an interview with the author.

served under Lieutenant Haughey and described him as a conscientious officer. The men were paid when on annual camp but also if they were part of the permanent cadre. Haughey, according to my friend, would insist on passing the young men's pay directly to their mothers because of his anxiety that the men would blow the money on drink. Even at this stage and prior to his arrival in politics, Haughey was dispensing welfare and was, according to my friend, popular with the mothers as a result.

Haughey won his scholarship to go to UCD where he studied Commerce. The UCD Commerce course is regarded as the best business degree in the country and today's business school in the college is highly placed in the world rankings. Garrett FitzGerald was also a student around the same time as Haughey in UCD. The two were known to each other. While there, Haughey appears to have been popular and was elected to the College's Commerce and Economics Society as its student Auditor. I served as a committee member on the C&E in the 1980s and it remained, even then, an item of significant pride to the society that Haughey was a previous Auditor. In fact, many joined the society precisely because of this during the recruitment period for clubs and societies in Fresher's week.

Haughey met his future wife Maureen at UCD. She also studied Commerce. The only other remarkable aspect to Haughey's early years was an incident in May 1945 on the occasion of Victory in Europe day, the celebration of the Allies' victory over the Germans in the Second World War. Trinity College Dublin had, certainly up to the 1940s, remained a bastion of Anglo-Irish, protestant and pro-British opinion. Even in 1916 the students had set up a force to defend the college against Pádraig Pearse and his republican insurgents. On Victory in Europe Day, students from Trinity had hung out the British flag or Union Jack on a flagpole facing from the front of the College onto College Green. Haughey, along with other students from UCD, went to the front of the college, where a Union Jack was burnt on a lamp-post outside. With Haughey during this incident, which apparently started a minor riot, was Seamus Sorahan who went on to become a very eminent defence lawyer and barrister. It is important to state these influences on the young Charles Haughey, as it was often pointed out, wrongly, in subsequent years and in some of the analysis following the Arms Trial that Haughey was not considered very deeply republican up to the Arms Trial. Haughey was, by the standards of his time, strongly patriotic and that is mirrored in his pastimes and involvements – the GAA, the FCA and a father who had a service record with the IRA at the time of Irish independence.

In the middle of the 1950s Haughey gave some insight into his own views about the situation in the north. According to Patrick Maume in his *Monograph on Haughey* for the Royal Irish Academy:

> *"In January 1955 Haughey was appointed to a party sub-committee on partition, and on 15 January submitted a memorandum (co-authored by George Colley) suggesting the Irish Government should sponsor guerilla warfare in Northern Ireland on the model of the covertly sponsored Egyptian campaign in the Suez Canal Zone. The memorandum argued anti-partition sentiment was increasing and Fianna Fáil should not relinquish it to the IRA."*[8]

This particular memorandum is all the more intriguing as an insight into both Colley and Haughey's thinking given their subsequent divergence of opinion over the covert action initiated by the Army after the outbreak in the North of Ireland in 1969.

In 1950 Haughey set up his own accountant's practice along with Harry Boland, whose father Gerald was a minister in the de Valera governments. Harry was named after his legendary uncle of the same name who had been Michael <u>Collins' best</u> friend and a leading member of the Fenian

[8] Maume, Patrick, *Biographical Monograph*, Royal Irish Academy, Dictionary of Irish Biography

Brotherhood serving on the Supreme Council of the IRB. Harry Boland had been shot in controversial circumstances in the Civil War, which followed independence. It has been suggested that Haughey's recruitment into Fianna Fáil was by two school friends, namely Harry Boland and George Colley. George Colley's father, Harry Colley, was the sitting T.D. for Dublin North East and another worthy of the Fianna Fáil scene. It has also been hinted that Haughey delayed joining the party until his father had passed away. Through the Boland and Colley connection Haughey was now moving in the elevated circles of Fianna Fáil. In 1951 he would marry Maureen Lemass and thus become hugely connected to the party through his father-in-law Seán Lemass.

The 1950s were a time of great urgency within Fianna Fáil. In 1948 Seán MacBride, a former Chief of Staff of the IRA, led an electoral challenge to the party, which galvanised a younger generation against the party. The Clann appeared more radical than Fianna Fáil who as the 1940s turned into the 1950s looked increasingly tired under de Valera. There was a sense that de Valera, far from helping the party, was in fact at this stage hindering its progress. Many of his ministers were very old, had been around a long time, and the Chief himself was developing the condition of blindness. The feeling within Fianna Fáil circles was summed up by James Downey in his biography of my father where he quotes from my mother Ann about the scene:

> *"When the Chief met the young senator's bride, he discovered to his chagrin that neither she nor her husband had any interest in the Irish language, de Valera's greatest love. (Lemass similarly had no interest in Irish. De Valera counselled him to spend his time in opposition learning the language, but Lemass preferred to read J.M. Keynes.) Ann for her part, found her social encounters with the party gerontocracy less than delightful. 'What struck me was how old all the people were! And how clannish!' Grandees like McEntee*

and Aiken would ask her such questions as 'whose daughter are you?' They assumed that her father had to be one of their own."[9]

Seán Lemass was a very ruthless man and not too prone to sentiment. It is noteworthy that two of the people he chose to help him re-organise the party in the 1950s, both Haughey and my father, ended up displacing high-profile, older TDs with deep connections to the party's founding establishment. In the case of Haughey, he was to end up taking a seat from George Colley's father in the election of 1957 and in my father's case the seat of Gerald Boland in Roscommon in 1961. Boland was a significant internal critic of Lemass over a number of years and my father was made a Parliamentary Secretary on his first day in the Dáil. Haughey, it is speculated, made his school friend George Colley a lifelong enemy by unseating his father. Boland was so senior within the party ranks, having fought in the 1916 Rising, he hardly even needed to visit the constituency, and for the most part was based in Dublin. Even though both Harry Colley and Boland would have been lifelong comrades of Lemass, the latter was anxious to rejuvenate the party's ranks and was well prepared to throw younger candidates like Haughey and my father in amongst them with his tacit support. To those facing the competition from the younger candidates, the support of Lemass was not perceived as tacit and engendered bitterness towards the Lemass protégées as much as towards Lemass himself. Lemass in effect was grooming his own leadership group. Lemass biographer John Horgan captures this in his seminal work:

"Later in the year Lemass was allocated an annual payment of £500 in expenses as director of organisation (£7,850 in 1997 terms), by which time the work of reorganisation had been well established throughout the country. He hand-picked an Organisation Committee, whose membership by 1957 comprised Kevin Boland,

---

[9]Downey, James, *Lenihan – His Life and Loyalties*, New Island Books, 1998, p. 34

Stephen Ennis, Charles Haughey, Kieran Kenny, Noel Lemass, Brian Lenihan, Thomas O'Connor, Alec O'Shea, and Eoin Ryan." [10]

Learning at the feet of someone like Seán Lemass was an opportunity of a lifetime. Lemass had been the organisational genius behind establishing Fianna Fáil in the 1920s. It was Lemass, rather than de Valera, who put in the hard miles driving around the country persuading leading members of the IRA to give up the gun and commit to democratic or party agitation instead. Here again he was at the same task in the 1950s, the second time round. This time the emphasis was on the recruitment of young people. When my father was in opposition between 1982 and 1987 I was often given the task to drive him to events around the country. We would talk a lot on those journeys. As we passed through various parts of Ireland it was clear to me that my father had an encyclopedic knowledge of the people who were active or engaged in politics. He would throw out the local names, histories and record of activism from memory. Most of this knowledge had been derived from his involvement in the Lemass re-organisation drive. Despite the support from on high it took both men, Haughey and my father, several attempts before they broke through into the Dáil.

Haughey in his early Dáil contributions reflects his enormous devotion to Lemass. He is, like his patron, a fan of economic planning and an opening up of Irish life to external investment. Haughey took an active part in economic and budgetary debates even prompting a compliment from the then Minister for Finance Jim Ryan that Haughey knew more about income tax than he did. Notwithstanding his undoubted brilliance and intellect, it had taken Haughey four attempts to get elected to the Dáil. Along the way he had been elected to Dublin Corporation as a Councillor and then, in humiliating fashion, had lost this seat. The lessons were not lost on the young Haughey. Once

---

[10]Horgan, John, *Seán Lemass – The Enigmatic Patriot,* Gill & Macmillan, 1997, p. 160

elected, finally and at last in 1957, he was to inaugurate a local constituency machine of his own, making it well-oiled, well funded and destined to elect and re-elect him time and again for the rest of his political career. The politicians of the earlier generation had largely eschewed constituency work and placed their re-election on the basis of their national work, as well at their track records in the struggle for independence. The likes of Haughey and the new people being brought in by Lemass were not taking anything for granted nor, in Haughey's case, leaving anything to chance. Haughey operated north Dublin like a ward boss and in this respect his subsequent political career may seem more comparable to one of the great Irish figures of the United States that came to define the notion of Tammany Hall. In the same way that Tammany Hall became a by-word for corruption and graft so too the career of Charles Haughey became infamous. Tammany in New York became identified with the political rise of the Irish and other immigrant groups. In the same or similar ways, Haughey became adept at associating himself with groups who felt themselves excluded from power, or who in social terms, had the doors of the 'powers that be' closed to them.

Bryce Evans makes the point that Haughey, early in his career, had become a vital cog, to tie up Lemass' efforts to outreach to Irish industry:

> *"The familial tie was undoubtedly very important. But, most significantly, Haughey represented the new ethic Lemass was keen to instil in Fianna Fáil: he was young and good at cultivating business contacts. During the 1950s Lemass came to realise the limits of protectionism and state intervention and encouraged the attributes of self-reliance and enterprise instead. As well as injecting a certain dynamism, this general transition would result in the emergence of 'less desirable types' in the party. But it was a gamble Lemass was willing to take in his efforts to shake things up."[11]*

[11]Evans, Bryce, *Sean Lemass – Democratic Dictator*, The Collins Press, 2011, p. 199-200

In the 1950s Haughey was put in charge of Comh-Comhairle Átha Cliath, a special central branch of the party based in Dublin, whose remit was to recruit fee paying associate members of the party. The idea was that it would allow people who for a variety of reasons could not take a formal part in the party's organisation. The proceedings of this central branch were well supported by top party brass and led to a swelling in the party's financial coffers. This was a kind of precursor to the infamous 1960s structure called *Taca*, that was to lead to allegations of closeness between Fianna Fáil and the business community.

Lemass was clearly keen to have business support for both the Government and Fianna Fáil. Indicative of this was the career trajectory of my own grandfather P.J. Lenihan who first came into contact with Lemass as a Revenue Official and was later enticed to leave the Commissioners and become involved in establishing a 'tariff protected' textile factory in Athlone in the late 1940s. They were to remain great friends. When my grandfather later set up the Hodson Bay Hotel on the lakeshore of Lough Ree, near Athlone, Lemass would often stay when he wanted to take a break. He would come and do a bit of fishing and relax in what was then a fairly informal, family-run, hotel. My grandfather became the first and only case of a father following his son (my father) into the Dáil. This later involvement in politics was also at the instigation of his friend Lemass. Not unnaturally, my father, Brian, was regarded almost as extended family by Lemass because of this prior friendship between Lemass and his father.

When my parents married in 1958 an invite to the reception in the Royal Marine Hotel in Dun Laoghaire was extended to Lemass but for some reason he was unable to attend. He sent his daughter Maureen instead and she came with her husband Charles Haughey. Noel Lemass (son of Seán Lemass) and his wife Eileen also attended given the family friendship. Both my father and Haughey were now heavily involved in politics at a family as well as a personal level.

CHAPTER THREE

RISING TIDE

In late June of 1963, President John F. Kennedy of the United States became the first serving President of that country to make a full state visit to Ireland. It was a memorable occasion, both for the Kennedy family, but more importantly for anyone alive at that time in Ireland. The visit summoned up a public outpouring of goodwill. For Irish people, the Kennedy visit was in some way a validation of where they were and where they had come from. Kennedy, in his own way, had become emblematic of the Irish struggle for success in the United States. He was the first Catholic of Irish ancestry to reach the Oval Office. In Ireland, Kennedy's ascent to power in American politics and the wider Kennedy family's rise to affluence stood out as something to aspire to. He was a role model of sorts for a great many Irish people.

There was a clear appetite for change in the country. Deep poverty and emigration were still features of Irish life. In his documentary about the Kennedy visit, *JFK in the Island of Dreams*, filmmaker Darragh Byrne makes the point that in rural Ireland there were still 200,000 farmers and their families trying to eke out a living from sub-subsistence farms of under 30 acres. 90% of these homes had no running water and a further 50% had no electricity. The exodus from the land was also being accelerated by the fact that there were now new, industrial, jobs in the towns and cities.

The narrator in the TV documentary underlines the above in the following way:

"At home in Ireland a quiet revolution is underway. Gone is de Valera's dream of a simple island people who speak an ancient Celtic tongue. Today's Irish are restless, anxious to take their place among the modern European nations. The monolithic structures of Church and State that have preserved the status quo for decades are now increasingly under pressure to change. Seán Lemass, a highly progressive statesman who embodies the new spirit of Ireland, has been Taoiseach since 1959. Under Lemass, Ireland's first Programme for Economic Expansion has been pushed steadily forward. In the years up to 1963 more than one hundred new industrial plants have sprung up around the country, creating thousands of new jobs."[12]

Lemass appeared on the front cover of the July 1963 issue of *Time* Magazine. It was an iconic moment indicating change was well in hand in Ireland. He and his younger ministers, including Haughey, were kicking off the dust of the past in a forthright and convincing manner. Lemass was great to work with. According to my late father Brian Lenihan, he let his young ministers get on with their own tasks. Haughey's reputation as a minister from 1960 onwards was of a diligent, reform-minded, politician. He carried out a wide-ranging law reform agenda at the Department of Justice and won admiration from its inveterate Secretary General Peter Berry who thought him able: "He was a joy to work with and the longer he stayed the better he got." The Succession Bill 1965, which would outlaw the practice

---

[12]JFK *In the Island of Dreams*, RTÉ Commissioned TV Documentary, 1993

whereby husbands and families could dispose of family property against the interest of the surviving wife, was ground-breaking legislation. It was a bill that women in particular were grateful for in terms of the development of their often-neglected rights in Irish life up to that point. It fell to my father to guide the Succession Bill through the Dáil and end the malign practices and machinations of families against the interests and well being of often, very vulnerable, widows. The Act was added to the statute books in 1965.

Haughey's period at the Department of Justice was not entirely about tidying up and consolidating legislation. He had other issues to deal with including a revolt in 1961 by the Garda Representative Association. When one of their pay demands was rejected the Garda Representative Body called a meeting at the Macushla Ballroom in Dublin, which the Garda Commissioner deemed to be illegal. The Minister was requested to dismiss eleven members of the force, which was duly done. The intervention of the Catholic Archbishop of Dublin, John Charles McQuaid, saved the situation and the reputation of the Minister, who agreed to McQuaid's request to have the men reinstated. Haughey had cultivated McQuaid over the years via copious visits to the Archbishop's Palace. McQuaid was a notorious conservative but Haughey had developed this uncanny ability to find allies in the most unlikely of places.

"When McQuaid lobbied Haughey to secure the banning of a novel by Edna O'Brien, he noted that the Minister had been shocked by its eroticism, as one might expect from a Catholic married man with a growing family. The publication of this memorandum in 1999 aroused comment about McQuaid's naïveté and Haughey's early-developing hypocrisy,"

according to Patrick Maume of the Royal Irish Academy.

In the Department of Justice, Haughey also won praise for his ability to finally bring to an end the IRA's border campaign. The Department of Justice has proven to be the graveyard of many a political ambition. Haughey appears to have thrived in that Department. His abilities and his qualification as both accountant and barrister obviously were of benefit.

Apart from his reputation as a reformer and speaker on economic issues, Haughey, according to Bruce Arnold, began to carve out a reputation in relation to the arts:

"Thirdly, he became interested in the arts and was supportive of a broad range of cultural developments, from traditional music, architecture, poetry and writing, to galleries and painters. He led the 'New Men' in the Government. They were himself, Donough O'Malley and Brian Lenihan, and they were associated with commercial and business interests that were regarded as responsible for getting Ireland moving again."[13]

The *Irish Times* journalist and writer John Healy went so far as to depict the triumvirate of Haughey, O'Malley and Lenihan as a kind of 'inner cabinet' for Seán Lemass. All three were very close to Lemass.

The journalist Raymond Smith puts it thus:

It was the time when Brian Lenihan and Donogh O'Malley, both made Parliamentary Secretaries after the General Election of 1961, formed a very close friendship with him. They had the panache and the flair that made him gravitate to them and they to him and the three became inseparable pals politically and socially. As Haughey himself would recall later – 'We were known as the Three Musketeers'.[14]

[13]Arnold, Bruce, *Haughey – His Life and Unlucky Deeds*, Harper Collins, 1993, p. 43

[14]Smith, Raymond, *Haughey and O'Malley – The Quest for Power*, Aherlow Publishers, 1986, p. 21

All three were to become well-known "men about town". They circulated between the Shelbourne Hotel, Jamet's – an exclusive restaurant at the time, the Hibernian Hotel on Dublin's Dawson Street and the old Russell Hotel on St Stephens' Green. The exploits of all three were greatly mythologised but the wildness of one of them, Donough O'Malley, was to be his own undoing. A heavy drinker, O'Malley was believed on one occasion to have driven his state car the wrong way down O'Connell Street and after being stopped by a Garda who asked him had he not seen the arrows, O'Malley replied that neither had he seen the Indians! Haughey was later to confess in an interview with Seán O'Rourke of the *Irish Press* that a lot of the 'fun of politics' had disappeared for him, at least, when Donough O'Malley died in 1968.

Another famous watering hole for people in these halcyon days was Groome's Hotel located near the top of Dublin's O'Connell Street.

The author and journalist James Downey takes up the story:

"Groome's Hotel was not only the best known but the most respectable of Dublin late-night drinking resorts, and it was at the height of its popularity in the fifties and sixties. The customers were politicians, chiefly, but not exclusively, of the Fianna Fáil persuasion; actors and directors from the Gate Theatre opposite; journalists, artists, intellectuals and writers, among them Peadar O'Donnell, Seán O'Faolain, and Kate O'Brien.[15]

In his memoirs, the well-known actor Peter Ustinov recites an incident where he ran into Donough O'Malley on his way down the stairs of the hotel complaining that he was late for a cabinet meeting.

---

[15]Downey, James, *Lenihan – His Life and Loyalties*, New Island Books, 1998, p. 41

Haughey had become a major player in the Lemass governments of the 1960s. The extent to which Haughey was coming to the nation's attention was obvious and well referred to in Bruce Arnold's book:

"Even as early as 1960, Haughey kept horses and rode to hounds. He was photographed at times wearing a top hat, but in any case always correctly turned out. He developed expensive tastes. He had a cellar of fine wines, dined frequently and lavishly in Dublin's best hotels, and seemed at pains to demonstrate his success in an ostentatious way, and to display quite clearly an association between wealth and power."

In 1964 a twist of fate assisted both Haughey and my father. The Minister for Agriculture, Paddy Smith got into a cabinet row with, amongst others, Lemass and the then Minister for Finance, Jim Ryan. Smith resigned on a point of principle but Lemass moved swiftly to out manoeuvre him and the potential for controversy by appointing Haughey to Agriculture as well as lifting my father from his position as Parliamentary Secretary to the position of Minister for Justice. It was done with such speed that the new promotions dominated the news media headlines rather than coverage of the resigning Minister. My own mother learnt of her husband's promotion from an evening paper while shopping in the centre of Dublin.

While confessing he knew very little about Agriculture, Charles Haughey was now in a hugely important ministry from a promotional perspective. He was only to last in the portfolio for 18 months. He was quickly confronted by the obduracy of the farming organisations when they staged a march on Dublin and camped outside his offices in a massive protest over their income. Haughey was not comfortable with the whole thing and the dispute was only eventually resolved by the Taoiseach, his father-in-law, who chose to settle things in the brief period he served as a caretaker Taoiseach while Fianna Fáil were ruminating about the successor to Lemass. Not withstanding his difficulties, the sojourn in Agriculture had burnished his credentials sufficiently for him to be considered a runner for the leadership of the party in 1966 when Lemass stood down.

Quite apart from his formal role in the Department of Agriculture, Haughey was given a role in directing the re-election of de Valera to the Presidency in 1966. This was a difficult challenge for the Government as the Presidency was seen to be above politics. However there was a need to campaign on de Valera's behalf. De Valera, as an incumbent, was constrained in how he could campaign without jeopardising the independence of the office as he had conceived it in his own 1938 Constitution. Lemass and the party engineered the 1966 Easter Rising commemorations in a way that gave great prominence to Eamon de Valera's role in the rebellion. In addition to this, the party managed to deny O'Higgins broadcast coverage on the basis that de Valera, as incumbent President, could not become involved in day-to-day political controversy. It was a bit of a ruse but it worked. The challenge from Tom O'Higgins of Fine Gael was serious and the result was to be close. Meanwhile, Haughey needed to settle his dispute with the farmers over milk prices. "As De Valera's national Director of Elections, Charlie pulled a political stroke and shored up the President's rural support by conceding on the milk price issue. In view of the narrowness of De Valera's subsequent victory, the concession quite conceivably made the difference between victory and defeat," according to T. Ryle Dwyer.[16]

Despite his obvious abilities, it was unlikely Haughey would become leader of the party in succession to Seán Lemass when the day came for Lemass to retire. His

[16]Dwyer, T. Ryle, *Haughey's Thirty Years of Controversy*, Mercier Press, 1992, p. 24-5

performance in two important ministries had earned him great credit. The writer John Waters bemoans the fact that Fianna Fáil did not in fact, select Haughey as their leader in 1966 stating, "Had Haughey come next, recent history might have been different, but the party lost its nerve, causing Haughey to become ingrown and stunted."[17] In reality Haughey was still somewhat head-strong in his attitude and regarded by many to be arrogant. That was my father's assessment when I asked him why Haughey had not made it then given his obvious success. There was also the hostility of the older and more traditionalist members of the party who took great exception to his enormous wealth and lifestyle. Lemass was famous for making the comment that economic growth had the effect of a Rising Tide lifting all boats. This rising tide of the 1960s had so far been kind to Haughey and risen his boat. As the sixties came to an end his seemingly inevitable climb to the top was to be severely tested.

Tim Pat Coogan, the Editor of the *Irish Press*, labelled Haughey and the crowd that he mixed with in the 1960s the 'Men in the Mohair suits'. These types of suit, along with cashmere and angora wool were deemed to be fashionable at the time. Mohair has its own sheen that added a certain glamour to a man's suit. The term stuck and was added to by the creation of *Taca*, the Irish word for support, a new structure dedicated to raising money for Fianna Fáil amongst those in business who were benefitting from the rising tide of economic growth. For a £100 a year subscription, business people were invited to events and given the opportunity to meet with ministers. When delegates to a later Fianna Fáil Ard Fhéis threatened to vote it out of existence, it was Neil Blaney as Party Treasurer who came to the rescue, emphasising its importance from a fundraising point of view.

---

[17]Waters, John, *Was it for This? – Why Ireland Lost the Plot*, Transworld Ireland, 2012

According to Kevin Rafter in his book on Neil Blaney "Some of the biggest names in Irish industry were subscribers to *Taca*, membership of which was heavily concentrated among those in the construction sector".[18] Like its equivalent in more recent years, the Fianna Fáil fundraiser at the Galway Races, *Taca* had brought the unwelcome attention of an emboldened media who, along with left-wing commentators, saw its drawing together of business and politics to be in some way sinister. Party traditionalists also had a problem with it but were most unlikely to come up with an alternative mechanism for raising election funds. Charles Haughey wrote the blueprint for the organisation of *Taca*, which was for all intents and purposes the importation of American-style fundraising into Irish politics. T. Ryle Dwyer writes:

> *"Taca was a 'fairly innocent concept' according to Charlie. In so far as it had any particular motivation it was to make the party independent of big business and try to spread the level of financial support right across a much wider spectrum of the community.*
>
> *Some members had previously been subscribing 'substantially more' to the party at election time than the £500 that would accumulate in* Taca *subscriptions, if the Dáil ran its full five-year term, he contended."[19]*

Blaney though not the initiator of *Taca*, was enthusiastic about it and attended many of its gatherings. According to Des O'Malley in his autobriography:

> *"Blaney was the party's self-declared champion of by-elections. He arrived with a team of workers from his Donegal bailiwick, the 'Donegal mafia.' They were tough boys, ready for a fight. In the 1960s they were by-*

---

[18]Rafter, Kevin, *Neil Blaney – A Soldier of Destiny*, Blackwater Press, 1993
[19]Dwyer, T. Ryle, *Haughey's Thirty Years of Controversy*, Mercier Press, 1992,p. 32-3

*election aficionados who travelled around the country
to organise local campaigns.*"[20]

The Blaney by-election machine was not confined, solely,
to activists drawn from his own constituency. People like
Albert Reynolds, publican Dessie Hynes and future Senator
Eddie Bohan got their first taste of national politics through
helping out in these by-election campaigns. The by-election
operation was particularly effective when Lemass was
still in the uncertain situation of presiding over a minority
government. Blaney was also creating his own myth. His
party organisation in Donegal was regarded as so slick it
became the subject of a noted study by U.S. based political
scientist Paul Sacks entitled *The Donegal Mafia: An Irish
Political Machine*. The book is required reading for those
interested in what is termed parish pump politics. It sets
out the influence and patronage networks established by
Blaney activists in Donegal. Blaney also would have been of
immense ambition and more senior to Haughey in the party
both by dint of years and service. The Blaney machine and
the Fianna Fáil organisation, thanks to *Taca*, was taking
on a very modern or American feel. My father, Haughey,
Blaney and others were giving this perception of the party
a big push in people's minds. There was this naïveté and
ruthlessness to the 1960s that made the era special. The
Cold War was at its height and the Men in the Mohair Suits
were not averse to throwing a 'Red Scare' into the equation
when it came to elections. The Labour Party were hardly
worthy candidates for such kind of smears but in the latter
part of the decade they began to attract an eclectic group
of intellectuals who were keen to assert that the 1970s in
Ireland would be socialist.

Haughey was powering away in government with
few denying his undoubted abilities. However he was
storing up media critics on a number of fronts. While in

[20]O'Malley, Desmond, *Conduct Unbecoming – A Memoir*, Gill & Macmillan,
2014, p. 31

the Department of Justice he had done many favours for friends, including Donough O'Malley, by arranging court sitting times so that the media would be absent and unable to report the proceedings. It was a stroke and one that annoyed media professionals who were depicted as lazy for not following these cases. His strong pressure on RTÉ over the Presidential election, involving de Valera, had seen him apply high-handed pressure on the station. There was also pressure applied to them over his dispute with the farmers that did not endear him to those at the helm in the national broadcasting station. That said, his career was flying and it was hard to see it falling apart.

A whole new world of possibilities was opening up for Ireland. According to the journalist Raymond Smith:

> *"It was the decade of the boom in ballads, of becoming acquainted with Ronnie Drew and the Dubliners and the Clancy Brothers and Tommy Makem and also of the advent of the big ballrooms of romance. America had nurtured Elvis Presley, England the Beatles – and now Ireland the Showband Craze. An English observer likened this booming industry to the leprechaun – 'a purely native product'."*[21]

However native, it was to make one Albert Reynolds a cash fortune and set him on his way to a late career in politics.

---

[21]Smith, Raymond, *Haughey and O'Malley – The Quest for Power*, Aherlow Publishers, 1986, p. 21-2

CHAPTER FOUR
SUCCESSION

The leadership contest within Fianna Fáil in 1966 was without precedent. There had literally been no such contest before in the party's history. Due to its origins in the War of Independence and subsequent Civil War there was a tight seal of discipline amongst the party members and its founders. Dissent was kept to a minimum and values of loyalty, military discipline and self-abnegation were seen to be more important than individual ambitions or careers.

In 1926, at the party's foundation, de Valera was the obvious leader, though the idea of setting up a new party was not his, but rather that of his life long devotee, Seán Lemass. The younger man had done the hard organisational slog in the 1920s, calling to those disaffected republicans who had survived the defeat in the Civil War but were still reluctant to consider involvement in politics, least of all become involved in party politics and attend the Dáil, the new Irish parliament created by the Treaty with the British following the War of Independence.

Seán Lemass had huge credibility with the remnants of the IRA who had come through the Civil War. De Valera, despite what has been said and written about him, was in the context of the civil war considered a moderate. Arch republicans who fought the treaty were sceptical about him and in particular his use of Frank Aiken to wind down the conflict. It was left to Seán Lemass to visit every parish and town in the countryside to mobilise the hard-headed IRA men to join the new party led by de Valera. Lemass was the quintessential IRA organiser and in a way a gruffer more ideological version of Collins. He was de Valera's alter ego and at the same time political hatchet man. He was also the man that kept the wartime economy of neutral Ireland on the road, despite the huge challenges of ensuring supplies and issuing rations for essential items to the population.

As the 1950s progressed it became more and more the case that de Valera was reaching the end of his tenure in office. In physical terms his eyesight had deteriorated and he was finding it difficult to keep up with the voluminous amount of cabinet and governmental paperwork. When it came to passing on the leadership from de Valera, Lemass was the obvious candidate. There was no leadership contest. Lemass had all the attributes of an old man in a hurry. He encouraged and groomed a whole team of younger politicians to fill up the party's ageing ranks, one of whom of course was my father the late Brian Lenihan Senior. Like an old chess master he moved his younger pieces into position carefully rather than clearing the ranks in one big manoeuvre. His cabinet changes were more gradual than sudden. His style of leadership was far less deliberative than that of de Valera. The latter was paranoid about splits, following his own experience in the civil war. De Valera's cabinet meetings sometimes took hours to come to a conclusion or decision. De Valera proceeded by way of consensus and talked the issues out to the point where people were exhausted.

Lemass preferred quick decisions and was more likely to pre-cook a decision that was to come before cabinet. On a few occasions he created controversy by allowing individual ministers to fly kites about potential decisions that were in the pipeline.

The greatest example of kite flying by one of the then ministers was Donough O'Malley's announcement of free secondary education. He discussed the matter verbally with Seán Lemass, as Taoiseach, but not with Jack Lynch the then Minister for Finance. O'Malley made the announcement via the newspapers and in effect made it a fait accompli. Free secondary education was probably the most important decision ever made by a government minister. It meant that no longer would parents have to scrabble for money or a scholarship, as with Haughey, to send a child to a good school.

The speed with which Lemass wanted to move sometimes ruffled the feathers of his colleagues, in particular those long-serving ministers who had come to power under de Valera and been around the cabinet table for a long time. Lemass had been cautious in easing out the old warriors who had soldiered under de Valera, preferring to do it over a series of changes in his ministerial line-up. He was not universally popular amongst his colleagues. Seán McEntee, for example, was a long term, intellectual, internal opponent coming from a much more conservative outlook in terms of social and economic matters. Prior to Seán Lemass' own departure from office there was only one member of the cabinet left from de Valera's original cabinet team and comrades, the ever-present Frank Aiken. Aiken was the Chief of Staff of the IRA who issued the 'dump arms' order which ultimately brought the Civil War to an end. He was hugely connected to de Valera and the suspicion of my father and others is that he was only left on in the cabinet because of his connection to de Valera. He was viewed as being de Valera's 'eyes and ears' in the cabinet both when de Valera remained Taoiseach and afterwards when Lemass took over.

Aiken became very important to de Valera towards the end of his period as Taoiseach as de Valera was, at this stage, significantly blind and depended on Aiken to mark his cards on the formal paperwork that comes before cabinet. Aiken paid regular visits to Áras an Uachtaráin in the Phoenix Park to take instructions from de Valera after de Valera had left government and become President. My father viewed Aiken as a bit of a stiff old gentleman and a bit devoid of imagination. Even after he was elected President he, de Valera, continued to take an active interest in the Government and frequently pushed his own nominees for promotion to or promotion within the Government. Little has been written of the extent to which de Valera continued to interfere in cabinet appointments. He generally favoured Irish speakers over others and ambitious ministers, seeking promotion, were not averse to making appointments for themselves with the President to impress him by speaking Gaeilge to him.

One instance of de Valera's interference in ministerial appointments saw my father lose out to Patrick Hillery as Minister for Foreign Affairs in 1969. My father had been told by Jack Lynch he was getting the position and had been groomed for such a role by Seán Lemass. De Valera apparently insisted that it go to Dr Patrick Hillery because of his Clare connection, de Valera's old constituency.

The de Valera-Aiken relationship was one of total trust. Aiken shared de Valera's love for the Irish language whereas Lemass was no big fan of the Gaeilgoiri tendency within the party. In fact he hardly spoke Irish, nor had he any great interest in doing so. My father was of a similar disposition to his mentor Lemass. In fact my grandfather made the point to him that one could get on, with the help of de Valera, if my father would only knuckle down and learn his Irish. A summer holiday was duly arranged for the Aran Islands for what turned out to be the sweltering summer of 1968. My father hardly appeared due to the pressure of his work and when he did it was to share a drink in the numerous shebeens around the main island. Not a lot of Irish was spoken or learnt.

As 1966 dragged on, Lemass started to casually forewarn some of his younger colleagues that he would be stepping down. While some expressed surprise at Lemass' seemingly rapid departure from office, my father, who dined with him quite a lot, was not as surprised as others at the time. He had been with Lemass at a function in the Shelbourne Hotel in Dublin where Lemass had a fainting spell. There was ample evidence that his health was not up to the strain of the job. His biographers suggest he was also anxious to hand over the reins of office, not just to let the younger crew take command, but also because he had not provided well for himself and was anxious to pick up a few directorships so that he could secure things for his wife. De Valera, while Taoiseach, had rarely if ever agreed to increase ministerial pay. This was a frequent complaint by ministers and TDs over the 1960s and into the 1970s. De Valera took a very austere and thrift-driven view about how politicians should be paid.

Lemass encouraged a number of the newer cabinet crop to consider themselves to be either leadership candidates or to have a role in who should be selected. Lemass initially told my father that he wanted to keep out of the succession stakes and stay above the whole thing. According to Bryce Evans:

"Lemass's resignation represented a tacit acceptance that his influence upon national development and economic recovery had been significant but – amid the winds of social and cultural change that the 1960s generated – was limited. Anxious to avoid accusations of nepotism, Lemass did not express a preference when meeting the three candidates for succession –

George Colley, Jack Lynch and Charles Haughey. He maintained an aloof stance in the unfolding drama, which was seen by most people as a clash between the slick, ambitious Haughey and the cleaner Colley."[22]

It does appear that Lemass had earlier sounded out both Jack Lynch and Patrick Hillery about the leadership, prior to his retirement, but both had been definitive in stating they would not run for it. As Jack Lynch put it himself:

"About seven weeks before he eventually retired, this would have been about mid-September 1966, Seán Lemass called me into his office and enquired if I was interested in succeeding him as Taoiseach. I told him emphatically that I was not, and he seemed to accept it."[23]

The net result of Lemass' decision to stay neutral in the contest for his successor was that two of the younger and most ambitious candidates emerged, namely, Charles Haughey and George Colley. The latter was only 18 months in the government but already something of a favourite amongst the old guard. Frank Aiken had taken a fatherly interest in Colley's career and the latter was fluent in Irish. Aiken would have favoured Colley because of his father's previous involvement and pedigree. In fact Aiken held it against Haughey that his father had been in the service of the Free State Army during the Civil War. Colley was also one of those ministers who attended at Áras an Uachtaráin to converse with de Valera. Aiken wrote to Lemass, stating, "As I see it, George would be the most acceptable to the party, but he could do with another few years of experience."[24] My father was adamant that Colley was way out of his depth and that Aiken had been

---

[22]Evans, Bryce, *Sean Lemass – Democratic Dictator*, Collins Press, 2011, p. 255

[23]O'Mahony, T.P. *Jack Lynch – A Biography*, Blackwater Press, 1991

[24]Horgan, John, *Seán Lemass – The Enigmatic Patriot*, Gill & Macmillan, 1997, p. 334

promoting him as a solo-run on his part and that the Colley candidacy had no benediction direct or indirect from de Valera. Donough O'Malley, the Minister who introduced free education in Ireland, was swift to declare his colours and became Haughey's campaign manager. The perception grew that it was going to be a Dublin or metropolitan face-off between Colley and Haughey. The media partly fed this momentum but neither man was considered of sufficient standing amongst the backbenchers and TDs whose votes decided the matter.

In fact, according to my father, neither was very popular at all. Kevin Boland, a member of the cabinet, confirms this, stating that, "There was no way that the party wanted a choice between Colley and Haughey, they were not going to have it."[25] In the clear vacuum that formed, both Boland and Neil Blaney conferred with each other and agreed that they would put their weight behind Blaney. At this stage the older members of the party were a bit shocked at the naked jockeying for position and canvassing that was going on. There were concerns about party unity, dissension and even complaints from some like Todd Andrews that Lemass had not made proper succession plans. According to John Horgan in his Lemass biography:

"The prospect of a two-horse race finally disappeared when Kevin Boland put forward Neil Blaney's name. Blaney's candidacy was inspired largely by a belief, which he himself shared with Boland, that the race between Colley and Haughey was a media creation. The three-way contest was dangerously unpredictable, and the only certainty at that stage was that neither Colley nor Haughey would withdraw in favour of Blaney."

The decision by Blaney to stand marked a distinct turning point in the contest. Lemass, amongst others, was becoming horrified at what they had seen to date. Kevin Boland states

[25]Rafter, Kevin *Neil Blaney A Soldier of Destiny*, Blackwater Press, 1993

that Lemass panicked on the basis that Blaney would beat the other two. This view was certainly my father's view also. Blaney had the pulling power and age to beat both Colley and Haughey. My father always said that while Lemass regarded Blaney highly, he saw him as an 'organisation man' and not the type of person to actually lead the party. Oddly this is a view which Blaney himself confirmed in his interviews for the Kevin Rafter biography where he states in an ideal world he would have wished for a number two role to another leader.

According to Jack Lynch, as indicated to T.P. O'Mahony:

"apparently, a group of old backbenchers went to Lemass at the stage when Neil Blaney became a candidate. They were worried that the party could be damaged by division and dissension. They strongly pressed the case for getting me to stand as the sole candidate, saying that I had clear majority support within the party, over and above the other candidates anyway".

Amongst those older deputies was my grandfather P.J. Lenihan, then a Dáil Deputy in his own right. He was prompted by Lemass to approach Lynch, along with other experienced deputies, to encourage Lynch to stand. Lynch, in later years, acknowledged the role played by my grandfather in getting him to stand. Lynch went back to his wife and asked her again. She had not been keen before but now relented to Lynch going forward. Lemass, having secured Lynch's agreement, now went about getting all of the other candidates to withdraw, starting with Haughey, then Blaney and of course Colley. The latter refused to pull out. My father viewed Colley's decision to defy Lemass on this request to pull out as gross arrogance on his part. Haughey and Blaney had taken instructions and were arguably far more qualified to be in the leadership race in the first place. Blaney, in particular, as he might actually have won the leadership contest.

Lemass biographer John Horgan says:

"According to Colley's later version of what happened, Lemass sent for him after he had got Lynch's agreement to stand. He told him that Lynch was in the race, that Blaney had withdrawn, and that Haughey had indicated that he would withdraw in favour of Lynch. When he asked Colley what his intentions were, Colley told him he wanted to talk things over first with Lynch – understandably, in the light of the earlier assurances he believed he had received from that quarter. He phoned Lynch, and they agreed to meet the following day, but was then astonished to hear on his car radio a report suggesting that Lynch would be elected unanimously and that all the other candidates had withdrawn."

Colley should have withdrawn but clearly felt overly confident about his prospects. The support of Aiken might have been decisive for him in deciding to follow through despite Seán Lemass' direct request. It may in fact have convinced him that he had in some way, tacit support for his bid, from among others de Valera himself. Aiken, my father always insisted, was on a solo-run in relation to his encouragement of Colley. However even stalwart members of the 'old guard' that would have been critical of Lemass, including Sean McEntee, were lining up behind Jack Lynch. Colley as was again borne out many years later in his leadership contest with Haughey in 1979 was not very good at calculating his numbers.

Haughey and Blaney, in that order, became the major beneficiaries from the ascent of Jack Lynch, however reluctantly, to the leadership of the party and Taoiseach of the country. Both had put their hats into the ring and withdrawn them before either man had their credibility irredeemably damaged by the contest itself. The potential for actual damage to his reputation had been considerable for Haughey at that stage. He was seen to be too much of a man in a hurry and there were question marks over his suitability and popularity. Blaney, in power terms if not in position terms, was greatly enhanced by the result. The actual vote result showed Jack Lynch getting 59 votes to Colley's 19. Colley had left a marker for the future. Consensus around the new leadership had been achieved. However, this uneasy consensus around Lynch was to be severely tested in the immediate years ahead. Lynch had far bigger egos in his cabinet than his predecessor. Outside of those who formally put their names forward for leadership were others who also would have an eye for the main chance and considered themselves contenders. Haughey had shown himself loyal, a good party man and prepared to put his head down when required by superior force. He had played a good game.

CHAPTER FIVE

JACK LYNCH

In the weeks and months after the leadership contest, Jack Lynch was often described as a 'reluctant Taoiseach'. It appeared people had formed the opinion that he was not fully committed to being leader of the country given the hesitancy with which he treated Seán Lemass' offer to become Taoiseach. But he was clearly the popular choice to be leader of his party once he threw his hat into the ring. The point, I suppose, is that he wasn't the first name that came into party members' heads when they thought about who should be leader. He was also described as a 'compromise' candidate for the position. Some of these descriptions rankled with both Lynch and his supporters. In particular, they resented the notion that he was some kind of temporary stop-gap or compromise solution to a leadership problem. Another reason for this early dismissiveness towards Lynch was due to the fact that while he had racked up significant ministerial experience in the departments of Education, Industry & Commerce and Finance, his performance, while steady, could hardly have been described as exceptional. There were a great many egos to rival his in his own cabinet. For starters, Haughey and Blaney had already achieved a certain fame, thanks to their efforts both at party and governmental level. Add to that figures like Donough O'Malley, my father, George Colley, and Seán Flanagan. Most of these could in fact been leaders instead of Lynch. Lemass, like Mao, had allowed a thousand flowers to bloom.

Haughey was the single biggest, cabinet level, beneficiary from the 1966 leadership contest to replace Lemass. Lynch appointed him to be Minister for Finance, a position from which he would be viewed as the leading potential successor to Lynch. This was a huge break for Haughey, but in many ways deserved, given his clear understanding of finance and business matters thanks to his professional qualification as an accountant. He had already made a name for himself as an effective party fundraiser. He was thought lucky to have got the break away from Agriculture, where as an urban deputy, he had been mocked a bit for his lack of experience in the area. In addition to that, he had been helped by Lemass' decision to intervene in his dispute with the farmers during the inter regnum between him standing down and the selection of a successor.

Meanwhile, Neil Blaney moved into Haughey's old job in Agriculture. Kevin Boland replaced Neil Blaney in the Department of Local Government, the department responsible for election constituency boundaries. In the 1960s Blaney, along with Boland, drew great and admiring plaudits for the knowledge and expertise they showed when it came to carving up the constituencies in such a manner as to optimise the Fianna Fáil vote. In a number of instances it was this carve-up that was deemed to be the difference between victory and defeat for the party. This right of the incumbent government of the day to decide the size and shape of the individual constituencies was only changed in the 1980s when it was finally handed over to an independent judicial commission to decide how constituencies should be split up to cater for population changes.

Colley remained Minister for Industry & Commerce. Given the strong figures that he had inherited in his government, it was natural that Lynch would confine himself to being a chairman-type figure with regard to the rest of his Cabinet. In essence, Lynch let his ministers get on with their individual portfolios without too much interference from his side. For those who harboured notions of replacing him, the idea that he was a temporary phenomenon took on a pleasing dimension. All they had to do, in a sense, was bide their time. Lynch of course turned out to be anything but a temporary phenomenon in leadership terms. As the journalist and author Tim Pat Coogan has said of him "Lynch was an Irish folk-hero". In many respects he had already become that before he even stood for the Dáil through his captaincy of the Cork Hurling team, his twin hurling and football All-Ireland medals, and his extraordinary feats on the playing field at club and county level. The fact that he was not definably from one of the big Fianna Fáil families and had no great legacy in the party meant he would become all the more popular with the public. Despite his achievements on the field and in the Dáil he had an 'ordinary man' appeal, which was substantial. Through both the GAA connection and the Cork connection he had personal contacts almost everywhere in the country. Lynch and his wife Máirín dedicated themselves fully to political life in a way that previous political leaders had not done.

For the modern reader it may be difficult to see those involved in politics, at an elected level, as being in some way glamorous. However in the 1960s the new generation of politicians like Haughey, Donough O'Malley, my father, Jack Lynch and George Colley had a certain allure or newness that captivated people. The media was diversifying its coverage of politics. It was not now reported in a straight reportage fashion. Small political gossip columns were beginning to start. The activities of Haughey, my father and O'Malley, in a social sense, were beginning to be reported with a degree of awe. Unlike the previous generation, the newer political types were more accessible and were party animals. The social columnist Angela

Phelan has written of the image of Haughey carrying his Dom Pérignon champagne bottle to a party somewhere in Dublin carefully wrapped in brown paper. John Healy, the journalist and writer, had begun his 'backbencher' column that contained all sorts of speculative mischief and 'nudge-nudge' reporting. Healy was to become a sort of official reporter to the brat pack of politics. I remember meeting with Healy, in his later years, and marveling at his knowledge of wines as we looked at what was available in the shops on a trip to Strasbourg. The sixties generation had much higher aspirations for themselves than their parents generation. The newer politicos were not as staid as their predecessors. They were seen to have power, but also a certain lifestyle of fame that added to their appeal. The country itself was getting wealthier and the politicians were basking in that new-found success. Lynch, because he was a handsome and athletic looking man, was a huge hit with women. They mobbed him whenever he came into a room. I remember, as a small boy, being brought to events that he appeared at. On one occasion I was literally swept under the tramping, ecstatic, feet of his female admirers. To my mind the behaviour of the women was a real mystery. It was a kind of populist fever with people reaching out to him, clapping him on the back and the women inevitably hugging and kissing him. Lynch was a natural, never embarrassed, always at ease in people's company and a big smile at the ready. He also had that rather steadying feature, also beloved by Harold Wilson in the 1960s, a tobacco pipe. The pipe was like a signature thing and made him look contemplative. It also harked back to an earlier generation where every man smoked a pipe. He had this kind of indefinable dynamism that people seemed to trust. At public events he would even break out into song, singing the traditional Cork anthem 'The Banks of my own Lovely Lee'. His eyes would often water up a bit, giving speeches, or occasionally even on television. The cynics used to state that these was whiskey tears, as he had a prodigious ability to consume alcohol and yet it would show little or no effect on him. I remember a dinner in the late 1960s where a bottle of whiskey was placed at his setting and had been fully consumed by the finish of the event. Fianna Fáil for its part, looked exceedingly happy with itself that it had found this kind of magic lantern replacement for the generation of de Valera and Lemass. Jack Lynch also lived a modest lifestyle, almost the diametric opposite to the life lived by Haughey. Lynch had worked in the civil service, as an official in the courts, and then decided to study law at night in University College Cork. He then went on to practice as a barrister.

Haughey, from his position as the new Minister for Finance, was also adding to the Jack Lynch magic lantern appeal. He had arrived in Finance at just the right time and was prepared to reap the fruits of the 1960s economic boom. In his 1967 budget he introduced a scheme that was to make his reputation and earn him the trust and support of the elderly for a long number of years to come. In what was seen as a very imaginative move he granted free travel to pensioners on all forms of public transport. The measure has been praised by foreign commentators as one of the most enlightened schemes in the world when it comes to the elderly. Haughey showed great sensitivity to the elderly in introducing it by ensuring that it was not restricted, in the sense, that everyone got this entitlement irrespective of their income. My own grandmother used the service it extended on a regular basis. An avid Bridge player, it allowed her, even in her last years, to travel around the country for competitions and gave her a lot of freedom she might not otherwise have had as a widow. It kept her active into old age. Haughey himself found it amusing that the scheme should be such an enduring and popular thing. A year of so before he died, I paid a visit to him in his home, Abbeville, in Kinsealy. I was in Malahide for a meeting and put a call in to see if he was in. When I rang the bell at his Gandon mansion he answered the door himself. I pointed to a huge pile of letters, tied up with string by the postman, which lay there beside the metal grate for scraping your boots. I expressed surprise that he was still getting such a volume of correspondence in his retirement. He laughed and said, "when they get the free travel they are so delighted they write to thank me". Apart from this scheme there were other items in the budget of 1967 that supplemented the free travel including subsidized fuel and electricity for the elderly. As his other budgets unfolded there was also a new measure to cover farming families on subsistence living standards. The introduction of what came to be known as small farmers dole did much to alleviate the distress faced by small holders.

Haughey also initiated a novel new scheme to encourage the Irish horse breeding industry. The tax concessions granted have made Ireland the third largest breeder of thoroughbred race horses in the world today. The success of this particular measure is best symbolised by the extraordinary success of Coolmore Stud in County Tipperary which is now the largest thoroughbred breeding operation in the world and its current owner John Magnier the most influential man in this global industry, even ahead of the celebrated breeder Sheikh Maktoum of Dubai who single-handedly saved the Newmarket sales in the UK, after the downturn, by continuing to purchase horses. Maktoum has also chosen to invest in Ireland and owns a number of stud facilities in the country. Sheikh Maktoum also supports a variety of local community efforts with generous funding. Haughey greatly admired Magnier and showed his appreciation by appointing him to the Senate years later when he became Taoiseach. The measure Haughey introduced effectively made horse breeding in Ireland a modern, innovative and expanding industry. It has brought some of the most famous and wealthiest horse people to Ireland where they have bought studs and made a myriad of private investments. Without Haughey's intervention the viability of this very Irish activity would have been very much in doubt.

Haughey was well-known, in a personal capacity, as a private collector of painting and sculpture. Perhaps, prompted by this private interest, in the budget of 1969 he advanced a significant tax concession to the arts.

This measure again became the subject of favourable international commentary. The country's policies were now being depicted as being very enlightened. The tax exemption for artists meant quite a few international writers, musicians and artists with large earnings moved to Ireland to avail of the tax benefit. The arrival of these well-known figures from the world of writing, as well as the rock industry, gave Ireland a strong image abroad from a visitor and investment perspective.

Patrick Maume of the Royal Irish Academy puts his progress in context:

"Haughey was now the leading Dublin Fianna Fáil Deputy, with particular responsibility for the party organisation in the city. He was Fianna Fáil's national Director of Elections for the 1965, and the 1969 general elections, the 1966 Presidential elections and the 1968 referendum on the government's unsuccessful proposal to change the electoral system."[26]

It was hard at this point to see anyone other than Haughey replacing Jack Lynch should he ever retire. Having first been depicted as a temporary or compromise leader he was now growing favourably into the role. In 1967 George Colley made a speech to a gathering of the Fianna Fáil party's youth wing referring to 'low standards in high places' that was generally taken to be a thinly-veiled attack on Haughey. Colley was beginning to take up his role as 'fly in the ointment' to Haughey's onwards and upwards progress.

The 1969 election was to confirm Lynch's independent appeal and his value to Fianna Fáil. The party's slogan, 'Let's back Jack', gave the new Taoiseach a first name

---

[26]Maume, Patrick, Royal Irish Academy Monograph, *Dictionary of Irish Biography*

familiarity with the voters. His countrywide tour generated a lot of excitement. Haughey, as National Director of Elections, made solemn noises about the left. Some very boisterous people in the Irish Labour party had come up with the slogan 'The 70s will be Socialist'. Fianna Fáil took this as a cue to unfurl the red flag and warn ordinary workers about Communism. It was the kind of 'red scare' that had been tried before and was to an extent helped on by loose talk from the Labour Party's new array of left-wing intellectuals like Dr Noel Browne, Conor Cruise O'Brien, David Thornley and Justin Keating. Haughey, in his address, seized on a promise by Dr Noel Browne to immediately nationalise the country's bigger industries. He said the ordinary worker was entitled to know what was in store for them if these "extreme left-wing social theorists are putting their doctrinaire solutions into effect". He continued that anywhere socialism had been introduced it had led to "lower living standards, depression, monotony."

The *Irish Times* correspondent Andrew Hamilton described Blaney addressing a rally in Donegal after coming on stage chewing gum and wearing dark glasses: "The 1969 election will go down in the books as the election of the hairy half-truth, of the television twisters and the comrades of Cuba."[27] Blaney in typical style was slapping on the red paint with a broad brush. Lynch ran a very populist campaign and was well-received wherever he went. The national tour took in a visit to a convent in every town. Lynch, complete with pipe, sipped tea with the nuns and to all intents and purposes might as well have been a saint in mortal form.

The supreme irony of the 1969 election was that while the Fianna Fáil vote did not actually go up, along with that of Fine Gael under Liam Cosgrave, they won a five-seat majority in the Dáil. "The scale of Lynch's victory in the 1969 election left his rivals restless," concludes the historian Joe Lee. According to T.P O'Mahony, "he could no longer be

---

[27]Quoted in Rafter, Kevin, *Neil Blaney – A Soldier of Destiny*, Blackwater Press, 1993

dismissed as an interim party leader, a mere stop-gap while the heirs apparent, and semi-apparent, fought out the real battle between themselves. They could now anticipate long years of thwarted ambition."[28]

Developments in the North of Ireland were soon set to become centre stage though few were to guess this in the immediate aftermath of the election. There had been some disturbing news from the North as the civil rights demonstrations got underway in 1968. There was considerable concern but not enough that it became an election issue in 1969. However in 1968 the outline of a future rift within the government was being hinted at. In November 1968 Neil Blaney made a speech to a party meeting in Donegal where he described the Prime Minister of Northern Ireland, Captain Terrence O'Neill, as leading a 'Bigoted junta'. The speech appeared at odds with the position taken by the Taoiseach Jack Lynch who was trying to re-create the Lemass tactic of reaching out to the Unionist government in the North. In fact at a subsequent Fianna Fáil national executive meeting Jack Lynch was at pains not to rebuke Blaney in any way stating that the border continued to arouse "deep feeling and emotions in people and it is natural that expression will be given to their emotions."[29] Blaney through a series of subsequent speeches was set to become the public, or ministerial, defender of the republican faith as things worsened in the North of Ireland. Blaney was, in my experience of him, utterly sincere in his commitment to and anxiety about the position nationalists were placed in up North. I remember vividly as a young boy meeting him in Donegal, near Malin Head. He took me on a drive right up to the border and pointed out the lights of Derry. It was the first time in my life I had seen the 'Six Counties'. He pulled up the car and let me walk a few steps north of the border.

[28] O'Mahony, T.P. *Jack Lynch – A Biography*, Blackwater Press, 1991
[29] Rafter, Kevin, *Neil Blaney – A Soldier of Destiny*, Blackwater Press, 1993

CHAPTER SIX

ARMS TRIAL

When you grow up in a political household you learn to bite your tongue. There are things you cannot say because they relate to your father's job in the government. You are never actually told what to talk about, or rather not to talk about, outside of the home. It is something you learn almost by osmosis.

My earliest and most vivid memory of how national events impacted on our home is of the outbreak of the violence in the north of Ireland in 1969. Catholics were being burned out of their homes. Loyalist mobs were on the rampage, aided and abetted by the Royal Ulster Constabulary. It was obvious to our young minds that our people were being picked upon. Feelings were running high. The nightly news on the old black and white TV fired out images of petrol bombs, flames and heavily armed British soldiers being pelted with stones as they made vain attempts to baton charge protesters and push them back. These nightly images were at odds with our own quiet domesticity but they appeared terrifying and ominous all the same.

One consequence of these pogroms against the Catholic population of the north was that the Irish Government decided to move to the assistance of these people who had been run out of their homes in the disturbances that began in 1969. Relief camps were set up along the border. Behind the scenes more serious plans were being made to provide the nationalist groups with weapons, so that they could defend themselves against a sectarian mob to whom the police or proper authorities were either turning a blind eye or actively helping. The arms importation would later become the subject of a huge political controversy as ministers were put on trial in what became known as The Arms Trial scandal.

To my mind, in our family home in Athlone, County Westmeath, these controversies were very present. Our mother sat my older brother Brian and I down and told us that things were very difficult in our Dad's job and that we were not to speak of discussions in the house, relating to his job, to those outside the house or family. It was the way Mum told us that added to the impact of it all. She sat us down, very deliberately, then kneeled down so that she could be at the same eye level as us. She said there would be people coming in and out of our home at different times of the night and that we were not to get up, become disturbed or speak of who had come when we went to school the following morning. We were already aware of a degree of coming and going from the house. Mum had only stirred our curiosity. We would creep into the front room to get a view of these cars and people that would come in and go away again. Dad frequently arrived home late and in the mornings the big, ministerial Mercedes would be gone to Dublin with Dad and his driver Joe before we had even risen for breakfast. He would come and go but we would not see him for what seemed an indeterminable amount of time.

I was six in 1969 and my older brother Brian was 10. Niall was four years younger than me and to a certain extent, because of his age, was unaware of the goings on.

We had good neighbours and one of these provided us with an alternative narrative to the events happening around us, which our parents were steadfastly tight-lipped about. Ivy Clancy, who lived across the way from us, would often mind us in her home. Her children were in and around the same age as Brian and I. Her husband was an army officer in Athlone, which of course was an army town. The barracks and soldiers loomed large in our daily life. You would see them in their green uniforms cycling to and from the barracks located on the western side of the town, which was divided by the river Shannon.

Our parents did not explain the nature of the controversy. Ivy Clancy was to be our assistant in interpreting these events. I remember one night watching the television and seeing the RTÉ News reporter announce that two government ministers had been fired, namely Charles Haughey and Neil Blaney. Another, Kevin Boland, resigned in protest at the sacking of the other two. There was a whiff of sulfur in the air. Things then got worse in that both of these ministers, along with an army intelligence officer called Captain Kelly and a Belfast IRA man called John Kelly, were put on trial for the alleged, illegal, importation of arms. This was the nightly discussion between Brian and I before tucking in for our sleep. We lay awake trying to make sense of this thing that our parents would not explain. Brian, who was very precocious, was to my younger years, well informed. He described the whole thing as a 'show trial' in a reference to Stalin's purge of loyal comrades in the Soviet Union. These were big words for me. Our neighbour Ivy Clancy also had very strong views on the subject. She was less concerned about the politicians on trial, but rather, the unfortunate army officer. She insisted on the man's innocence and kept referring to 'poor Captain Kelly and his family'. Her view was much less complicated than Brian's view and strengthened my conviction on the matter because her husband Bill was an army officer. Soldiers and officers were held in high esteem in those days in Athlone. Ivy also felt those on trial were right to be importing guns so as to save 'our people' in the north.

Around our own house Brian and I never mentioned our separate education on these matters, from Ivy Clancy, in the company of our parents or the company of people who would come and go through the house. To their understanding we knew nothing of what was going on. But every night Brian and I discussed the latest outrage in the north or development in the, by then infamous, Arms Trial. It was like the latter had replaced our more traditional habit of trying to frighten each other with chilling ghost stories. It turned out that our parents' paranoia about talk emanating from the house was very real. My father, despite being an important minister, was in a sense under suspicion as well as under surveillance. My father in this period rarely spoke his mind on the phone. Mum was also under instructions not to talk on the phone. The Secretary of the Department of Justice, a Mr Peter Berry, had decided to put quite a few members of the government under watch. Family members were told to act on the assumption that he had placed wiretaps on our home. Berry had become a sort of J. Edgar Hoover of Irish life, attracting adjectives such as overbearing, bullying, paranoid and that was often from people who had worked directly with him down the years. He maintained a book that was limited circulation to all relevant ministers that outlined in detail the intelligence gathered by the state on republican or IRA subversion as well as the activities of far left groups. Berry had an encyclopedic knowledge of the subject matter. He had carried out this task for the best part of 30 years. Many, including my father, believe he had been left too long in the same job. The former Taoiseach Garret FitzGerald referred to him as 'A strange man, a very strange man'.[30]

---

[30]Quoted in article by Brendan O'Connor in the *Irish Independent*, 06/05/2001

There was all this talk about civil war and even a potential *coup d'état* within the state. My father's position on all of this was rather more ambiguous than we fully understood at the time. He was a good friend of both Haughey and Blaney and as such had come under suspicion by his own leader, the Taoiseach Jack Lynch. So our father had good reason to keep his head down and ensure there was no loose talk coming from home that would only jeopardise his position within the government. My father tried to act as a peace broker between the two warring factions in the government and in the party. He was not always thanked, and to a certain extent, his friendship with Haughey cost him dearly in terms of subsequent ministerial promotion under Lynch. He was never fully trusted by the faction around the Taoiseach though he had acted in a loyal fashion to prevent the party being split at a very difficult time. Some of those gathered around Blaney felt that my father was sitting on the fence.

Years later when I went to college in University College Dublin, I would get to know one of Captain Kelly's daughters. It was clear the controversy and false accusation levelled at her father had scarred the family for life. It was not an easy thing to live with. In the 1980s I got to know Captain (Jim) Kelly very well. I resolved, many years later, when a member of the Dáil, to help him clear his good name.

The public files, when opened years after the Arms Trial, initiated a further controversy regarding proposed changes to the evidence of the then Head of Military Intelligence. It was not just a murky business but very dirty business indeed. The only person who emerges with credit is Captain Kelly whose book *Orders for the Captain* remains the only first-hand account of these events. What is clear from his account is that the Irish government set out to train and provide weapons for nationalists in the north, including members of the IRA, and when this emerged they hung the army officer out to dry. The politicians recovered. With the exception of Boland, they all kept their seats. Haughey went on to be Taoiseach in 1979. Captain Kelly had to wait more than 30 years from this date to clear his name. After his death, the then Taoiseach Bertie Ahern put in on the record of the Dáil that Captain Jim Kelly had done nothing wrong.

The Arms Trial was a defining event for both the party my father belonged to but more importantly for the country as a whole. The then Taoiseach Jack Lynch famously insisted that we, in the republic, would not 'stand idly by' while nationalists in the north came under attack. The reality was quite different. The attempt to intervene, by way of supplying arms, proved costly. In effect the uncovering of the attempted arms importation had the effect of splitting the country and the aftermath of the controversy surrounding the importation made the then government and subsequent governments far less amenable to intervention in the north. The denial in the early years of the troubles of the legitimate right of the Irish government to a say on what happened in the north meant that nationalists, both of the constitutional kind and those supporting the IRA, claimed that they had been abandoned. There is some evidence to suggest that the leaking of the arms importation may have been prompted by the British intelligence services who had early knowledge of attempts to purchase weapons on the continent by the Belgian-born Albert Luykx. Luykx had a restaurant in Dublin and was regularly congratulated by ministers on the work he was doing while they were dining at his establishment. Even George Colley did so on one occasion.

London would have been concerned at the ability of the Irish government to mobilise U.S. opinion in a manner hostile to British interests in the conflict. Captain Kelly, in my many conversations with him, in later life, was convinced that one purpose of the controversy, from a British perspective, was to reduce the Irish capability to respond.

With the outbreak of hostilities, riots and pogroms in the North, the cabinet was called back for an emergency meeting. On 13 August 1969 the Taoiseach Jack Lynch invoked his rights as Head of Government to make a live broadcast on RTÉ television. In his address he declared that the 'Irish government can no longer stand by and see innocent people injured and perhaps worse'. In the original draft the word 'idly by' had been referred to. The statement from Lynch was seen as hard-hitting as it took in the lack of legitimacy of the RUC police force, the futility of a British army deployment in the long term and the need for a UN peacekeeping force to be sent to the six counties of Northern Ireland. In a subsequent interview Neil Blaney stated, "That speech was composed word for word, every comma, every iota, as a collective cabinet speech. It was not Jack Lynch's speech, made on behalf of his government. It was a Cabinet speech, made by Jack Lynch."[31] At the Cabinet table Blaney, Kevin Boland, Jim Gibbons, Seán Flanagan and my father all called for the initial statement suggested by Lynch to be strengthened. The statement created the distinct impression that the Irish government was about to make a military intervention in the north.

In the years after the Arms Trial there has been an attempt to depict the real issue as being one of a power struggle within the government with regard to policy in the North with Jack Lynch being outflanked by stronger personalities like Blaney, Haughey and others. The reality was he was prepared to sub-contract out policy in this area to both the Sub-Committee and these stronger personalities. There were tensions within Lynch's government about the North. Blaney stated in a Donegal speech made in Letterkenny's Golden Grill in December 1969 that if the nationalist

[31]Rafter, Kevin, *Neil Blaney – A Soldier of Destiny*, Blackwater Press, 1993

population continued to come under attack then 'force' could not be ruled out. The speech was at odds with Jack Lynch's more conciliatory tone. However, notwithstanding these tensions, Lynch was still content to allow Blaney and others get on with their work. Kevin Boland actually resigned from the cabinet in frustration only to be persuaded by President de Valera to withdraw this his first resignation. My father's view was that Lynch was weak, in terms of his management of the cabinet, but also on the northern issue, and quite content to allow others make the running until things went badly wrong. Albert Lukyx, the Dublin-based Belgian businessman, who was asked to help out in contacting arms dealers on the continent of Europe was being clapped on the back by ministers he had not met before, that he met casually around Dublin. My father apparently, amongst them, stating that he was doing great work for Ireland.

In February 1970, the Minister for Defence Jim Gibbons had ordered the army to make contingency plans. This directive came as a directive from the government. The idea was that Irish troops would make limited incursions into the North as it was considered completely impossible for the army to take on the British Army in open conflict. Members of the IRA and Citizens Defence Committees in the north were drafted into the FCA and given training at Fort Dunree Camp in County Donegal. Clearly this training would have to be followed with the provision of weapons. The view was that a limited incursion by the army would also have to be accompanied by the activation of civic defence organisations, in particular Belfast, where Catholics facing pogroms could not be defended by an official or Irish Army presence. Many years later, as a journalist covering the peace process, I came across a number of IRA Commanders who had received the Irish Army training in this manner at Fort Dunree. All of them were very glad of it and some relayed to me that it, the training, was far more effective than the training they subsequently received in places as diverse as Libya and Zimbabwe. The officers in charge, they said, were highly motivated and the training very practical and designed to optimise the amount of destruction they could visit on the North with limited and locally sourced materiels. The various delegations that had visited Dublin and spoken to ministers had all asked for guns, including Gerry Fitt, a moderate and subsequent leader of the SDLP. "In a doomsday situation, the Irish Army planned to enter either Derry or Newry, and hold until such times as a third force arrived, an international force such as the United Nations," according to John Kelly, a founder of the Provisional IRA and co-defendant in the Arms Trial. [32] After the Arms Trial and many years later I got to know John Kelly very well. He was a friend of my father and joined the local Fianna Fáil Cumann in Blanchardstown when living there. He was of the view that everyone who needed to know about the arms importation knew, including the then Taoiseach Jack Lynch.

In addition to this, at one point, as things escalated, the Irish Army were ordered to deposit 500 hundred rifles to Dundalk Barracks in readiness for a full distribution of these to the civilian population North of the border should the so-called 'doomsday' scenario arrive. In the interim, plans were about to be made to get weaponry that would not be traceable to the Irish government. Army intelligence in the person of one Captain Kelly were to be given this role. He was essentially tasked with mounting a secretive, covert, operation of state whereby few if anyone was to be allowed to know that the Irish state would be actively intervening to protect nationalists north of the border and undermine efforts by the incumbent powers that be there to suppress them.

One significant move was a decision by the Irish cabinet to create a four-member cabinet sub-committee on the

[32]*The Detail,* Belfast based investigative news and analysis website

situation in the north which contained the Minister for Finance, Charles Haughey, the Minister for Agriculture Neil Blaney and two other ministers (Joe Brennan and Padraig Faulkner) both of whom represented border county constituencies. The committee took on tasks as diverse as propaganda, weapons purchase and liaison with community defence organisations, a kind of euphemism for the yet to fully emerge Provisional IRA. This committee rarely met as a group but rather took its decisions informally as and when ministers met each other. Haughey and Blaney were the driving forces. The deliberate decision to include Haughey was to ensure Department of Finance support for anything that was decided. Haughey also had knowledge in relation to Northern Ireland, as well as having co-authored with George Colley the policy memorandum back in 1955, which anticipated what was now being contemplated — unofficial, deniable, arming of insurgents north of the border. It is clear also, that the inclusion of only border county ministers, apart from Haughey, was to ensure it looked like a sub-committee that was only addressing issues of humanitarian distress. "I have never seen a Government decision that was drafted in such wide terms,"[33] was the verdict of Charles H. Murray, Secretary of the Department of Finance, after the event. Both the wide remit given to the sub-committee and the fact that the Department of Defence and the Department of Justice were not included on the committee makes it all the more likely it was designed that way to achieve its clandestine purposes. It was the CIA in the 1960s who coined the phrase 'plausible deniability' for situations where senior officials or political people were deliberately not included in the full detail of clandestine operations so that if they went wrong they could be denounced or it could be stated that those in higher authority had no actual knowledge of the operation. There

[33]Dwyer, T. Ryle, *Haughey's Thirty Years of Controversy*, Mercier Press, 1992, p. 137

is a great deal of this element to the way the importation of weapons for use north of the border was arranged. The Taoiseach Jack Lynch was clearly happy to go along with these arrangements and left it to the committee members.

My father avoided speaking about the Arms Trial in subsequent years but when he did he was adamant that the whole government was aware of what the committee and Captain Kelly were doing, in other words that guns were to be acquired for use in the north. Indeed Captain Kelly, according to my father, was a familiar figure around government buildings, ministerial offices and the Dáil generally. He found it both convenient and quite wrong for Jack Lynch to assert that the work of the committee had come as a surprise to him. For Lynch not to have known about what was going on would be equivalent to the Taoiseach of the day being asleep at the wheel of state. Micheál O'Móráin, the then Minister for Justice had been in bad health and drinking a great deal. It is suggested that O'Móráin had his eye off the ball with regard to matters in his department and therefore did not exercise any degree of control over Peter Berry whom Des O'Malley states was in *de facto* terms acting as Secretary General and minister. Berry amassed huge surveillance evidence of the attempted importation of weaponry from his Garda security and intelligence sources, becoming more paranoid with the passing day and with no minister to fill him in on the wider political support for the importation and the need for discretion on the whole business. It may even be the case, my father once suggested to me, that Berry was quite deliberately left out of the loop on the whole business, precisely because the operation itself was about giving weapons to people he had spent a lifetime pursuing from his security perch in the Department of Justice. O'Móráin insisted that he had kept the Taoiseach Jack Lynch informed of developments with regard to Captain Kelly's activities.

There are many examples, worldwide, from accounts of state-sponsored covert operations, of confusion between rival or competing security arms of the state. In the 1990s, as a working journalist I acted as an informal intermediary for Albert Reynolds, as Taoiseach, in the early phase of the peace process. One difficulty for him on occasions was that the Special Branch were, in many instances, intensifying their surveillance of key people both in the IRA and those liaising with them. This gave him, Albert Reynolds, valuable additional insight or intelligence but at times could also prove awkward.

Peter Berry had reason to be paranoid. Captain Kelly was in October of 1969 meeting with leaders of the IRA in a hotel in Bailieboro in County Cavan. Though in hospital at the time Berry is adamant that he told the Taoiseach Jack Lynch of the Special Branch reports about the Bailieboro meeting: "I told him of Captain Kelly's prominent part in the Bailieboro meeting with known members of the IRA, of his possession of a wad of money, of his standing drinks and of the sum of money – £50,000 – that would be available for the purchase of weapons."[34] This is important as the Special Branch at the time had two senior level informants or moles within the IRA. Jack Lynch denied this conversation took place with Berry. However it is quite clear that it did as Colonel Hefferon, the Head of Military Intelligence, was to hear of it directly from Jim Gibbons, the Minister for Defence, who sourced the information to the Taoiseach. The point here is that Lynch knew much earlier than he insisted that weapons were to be purchased for use in the north, presumably by members of the IRA. This and other testimonies underline that the weapons purchase and importation has all the characteristics of an undercover operation by the state.

In his book, *Destiny of the Soldiers*, Dr Donnacha Ó Beacháin makes reference to the government directive

[34]Ibid, p. 39

issued to the army by then Minister for Defence Jim Gibbons:

> *"This directive, the fruit of previous Government deliberations, was dictated by Gibbons in the presence of the chief of staff, Lieutenant-General Seán Mac Eoin, and the Director of Intelligence, Colonel Michael Hefferon.*
>
> *The government directs that the army (1) prepare to train the forces for incursions into Northern Ireland (2) make weapons and ammunition available and (3) make gas masks available."*[35]

O'Beacháin comments that the directive demonstrates beyond doubt that the provision of arms for distribution in Northern Ireland, when the government felt the situation warranted it, was official policy.

The idea that Captain Kelly was operating either outside his remit or outside the law is patently absurd. In fact he was receiving instructions from arguably the three most influential members of the cabinet; Charles Haughey, Minister for Finance, Neil Blaney the key mover on the cabinet sub-committee on Northern Ireland and finally his own Minister for Defence Jim Gibbons who was briefed at every step of the way, if not by Captain Kelly, then by the Army's Head of Intelligence Colonel Michael Hefferon. The involvement of Hefferon in the arms importation destroys any argument that somehow rogue elements had taken over government policy and were importing guns. Captain Kelly and his family have also pointed out many times that the Minister for Defence Jim Gibbons was in many respects more hawkish about the situation in the north than even Blaney or Haughey.

Haughey, for his part, was not passive in his involvement, holding meetings in his home at Kinsealy with key IRA figures as well as the Head of Army Intelligence Colonel

[35]O'Beacháin, Donnacha, *Destiny of the Soldiers*, Gill & Macmillan, 2010

Hefferon. Haughey's brother, Jock Haughey, was also, along with John Kelly from Belfast, part of a number of visits to the UK where attempts were made to meet with arms dealers. Peter Berry from his vantage point in the Department of Justice spoke to Haughey at one point about the importation. Haughey asked that the shipment of weapons be allowed travel immediately to the north once they had been landed at Dublin Airport. Berry kept assiduous notes of his conversation that were published, years later, thanks to the excellent investigative journalism of Vincent Browne and *Magill* magazine. The Berry Diaries series in *Magill* made for riveting reading. Berry asserted that matters could not have gone on for so long without the Taoiseach's knowledge unless he was turning a blind eye. Permission to land the cargo of weaponry was refused and the importation cancelled once the Department of Justice and the Special Branch indicated they were going to seize it.

Writing in *Magill* magazine, Vincent Browne states:

"Berry was in a quandary. As far as he could see, two Ministers, Haughey and Blaney, were involved in an illegal arms importation; the Minister for Defence Gibbons, was also implicated: his own Minister had failed to keep the Taoiseach adequately informed and had neglected to follow through on information given to him; and the Taoiseach himself seemed disinclined to do anything about the grave threat to the security of the state".[36]

Berry went to President de Valera who told him to raise the matter in person with the Taoiseach Jack Lynch.

Some of the arms dealers that Captain Kelly had been dealing with had connections to British Intelligence. They were now aware of what the Irish government was planning. Berry was aware that British Intelligence knew

---

[36]*Magill* Magazine, May 1980 edition

and told Jack Lynch as much. Even at this late stage Jack Lynch was anxious to keep the whole matter under wraps. He spoke to Haughey and Blaney, then told Peter Berry he had done so and that both had assured him there would be no repetition and that the matter was now closed. The Taoiseach Jack Lynch, in order to stave the issue off and presumably pacify Peter Berry, proceeded to request the resignation of O'Móráin as Minister for Justice. He went quietly, with the media being told it was a case of ill health.

As stories circulated about the purchase and attempted importation of the weaponry, Liam Cosgrave, Leader of the Opposition, was the subject of a tip-off, widely believed to be someone senior in the Garda Síochána at the time. It could as easily have come from someone within the Department of Justice. When he failed to get newspapers interested in running the story he approached Lynch on May the 5th 1970 naming the various people involved; Haughey, Gibbons, Blaney as well as the Military Intelligence officer involved. Lynch had no further room to wriggle out of the controversy and that evening requested the resignations of both Haughey and Blaney which, when they refused, led to them being sacked. Given that Jack Lynch had earlier spoken to the two ministers about the matter before the Cosgrave approach, his speed in now asking for their resignations is all the more surprising. "While we cannot be absolutely sure of this, it seems that the 'Leak' to Mr Cosgrave occurred after Mr Berry had been informed by the Taoiseach that he was not going to fire the two ministers," says Vincent Browne, who also points out that it may have been someone within the Department of Justice that Berry spoke to about the matter. In my view Berry himself cannot be ruled out as the author of the leak to Liam Cosgrave. His paranoia levels were at such a height it is plausible he could have done this through a proxy of some kind. Berry appeared to be puzzled and disappointed at the attitude of the Taoiseach to the arms importation. Berry was a big fan of Charlie Haughey, declaring him to have a brilliant mind, but even he seems to have been duplicitous towards him in not telling him of his own involvement in the matter as the importation developed. In other words Berry was sharing information with Haughey but Haughey was letting on he knew nothing of the arms importation.

Meanwhile, communication between the Taoiseach and his ministers had been fraught during this very compressed time period. Haughey, on the eve of his budget day announcement speech, fell off his horse in a riding accident. The Minister for Justice was intermittently ill at various points in the building crisis. Berry himself also had a health issue as things were coming to the boil.

Kevin Boland, deeply unhappy at the treatment of Haughey and Blaney, resigned from the government as did a Parliamentary Secretary, Paud Brennan. Within a very short space of time, three senior ministers and a junior minister had been exited from the government. The arms importation was fast to become the scandal of the century in Irish politics. There were open ructions in Fianna Fáil. The Dáil went into over 37 hours of continuous sitting to discuss the crisis. At the Fianna Fáil parliamentary party meeting Haughey and Blaney supported a unanimous motion that upheld the Taoiseach's right to remove them. A veneer of unity was maintained with Haughey, Blaney and Boland all voting again for the government at the end of the Dáil debate on the matter. Haughey declared he accepted the Taoiseach's decision stating "the unity of the Fianna Fáil party is of greater importance to the welfare of the nation than my political career".

It is not clear at this point why Jack Lynch opted to put those involved on trial in the courts. My father always said that the main person pushing for a prosecution was George Colley. In all of the discussions around the issue with his ministerial colleagues my father said it was Colley more than anyone else that wanted people put on trial. The fact of the matter is that this was both a legal and political call. My father told me that the lawyers around the cabinet table argued against a policy of prosecution. There were sound political as well as legal reasons why a prosecution of those involved might not work and in fact rebound on the government. In those days the cabinet met for a period before the actual formal cabinet sessions began as a political group without officials and note takers being present. Ultimately the Attorney General, at that time, the law officer to the government made the formal decision to send the matter forward for prosecution.

Neil Blaney, according to my father, chose the right legal option in having the matter heard in the first instance in the District Court. His legal representatives succeeded in having the case thrown out of court without it going forward to a formal jury hearing. Haughey, Blaney, Captain James Kelly, Albert Luykx and John Kelly went straight to a Higher Court. My father always maintained that this was either hubris on their part or simply bad legal judgement. They too could have taken the avenue pursued by Blaney. In another irony, none of those who stood in the Dock, nor indeed the prosecution chose to bring Blaney into the trial as a witness. In any event the first trial was set to fall apart when the trial Judge, the then President of the High Court, declared a mistrial when accused of being unfair by the lawyers defending the accused five men. Many in legal circles have concluded that there was widespread unease amongst the judiciary themselves about the political character to the trial. In fact some have suggested that some very serious judges were quietly advising Haughey on his legal rights in his home in Kinsealy. In any case, Irish courts have always frowned on the notion of conspiracy charges given their origin and legacy in British colonial days.

The first trial was in huge difficulty anyhow after the evidence of Jim Gibbons as Minister for Defence and then the evidence of Colonel Hefferon. Years later Frank Fitzpatrick, Captain Kelly's lawyer, was to tell of a meeting he had with the former Head of Military Intelligence on the morning of the actual Arms Trial:

"I met him in the main hall of the court, a tall dignified person, who said to me 'I spent two hours in the church this morning and I am not going to commit perjury. I have to tell you that your client is telling the truth.'"[37] Gibbons told this trial that he had in fact been informed by Captain Kelly of his intention to seek weapons for the people in the north. This struck to the heart of the State's case as now it was beyond doubt that Captain Kelly was acting under direct supervision of the minister and government. It is clear that both Hefferon and Gibbons were being pressured to give evidence that was hostile to the defendants and in both cases were reluctant to go along with it.

"Hefferon's testimony was devastating. He established that Captain Kelly had not acted independently but with the knowledge and approval of Hefferon himself. Moreover, he added that, as Director of Military Intelligence, he had reported directly to the Minister for Defence on a regular basis and kept Gibbons fully briefed on Captain Kelly's activities. Indeed he testified that he told Gibbons that the Captain was going to Frankfurt in February 1970 to make inquiries about purchasing weapons."[38]

A second trial then proceeded under a different judge. The jury came to its decision quickly with Haughey leaving the court a free man. He was understandably jubilant and a little defiant: "I think those who were responsible for this

---

[37]Quote given to *The Detail*, a Belfast based investigative news and analysis website

[38]Dwyer, T. Ryle, *Haughey's Thirty Years of Controversy*, Mercier Press, 1992, p. 47

debacle have no alternative but to take the honourable course that is open to them." Taking the honourable course is a euphemism in political speak for someone to resign. His comments were sharply focused on Jack Lynch. If he was looking for Lynch's resignation it would not be forthcoming.

Haughey had played for high stakes in the trial itself. His line of defence was at odds with that of the other defendants. They insisted that they were merely carrying out government policy in attempting to import the weapons whereas Haughey insisted in maintaining the clear fiction that he as Minister for Finance did not actually know what was contained in the consignment being ordered by Army Intelligence. It was a strange line of defence on his part but clearly dictated by his desire to keep himself alive within the political system. The verdict itself had brought him a form of moral vindication but he was, despite his obvious ambition, about to become a sort of persona non grata in Fianna Fáil, a mere presence at the feast, someone to be avoided at all costs.

The then Taoiseach Jack Lynch clearly knew of the Arms importation, but when the consequences became clear, backed off and decided to blame the entire fiasco on those ministers, and Captain Kelly, who had played such an active part in the attempted arms importation. He had thrown them to the wolves while he remained unscathed by the wide repercussions of what happened.

CHAPTER SEVEN
WILDERNESS YEARS

With the disappearance of four ministers from the government, Jack Lynch was not slow in filling the vacancies and chose people who would be loyal to him. His Chief Whip, Des O'Malley, was put into the Department of Justice to replace Ó'Móráin. Many might have felt that Des O'Malley would have fitted in well with Haughey given that his uncle, whom he had succeeded as TD in Limerick, was such a big fan of Haughey. Quite the opposite, in fact. O'Malley gravitated towards Jack Lynch.

O'Malley first entered politics in the 1968 by-election in Limerick East. My father had backed him in preference to Hilda O'Malley, Donough's widow. Neil Blaney was furious with my father and told me so years later. Blaney was trying to get Hilda to run and was offering her the nomination in the front room of her home after Donough's funeral when a friend overheard and informed him that my father was offering the chance to run to Des, located in the back kitchen. My father did not like the practice that existed in those days of standing widows when there was a by-election and he was impressed with Des, then a young solicitor. Des O'Malley won the by-election but in the subsequent general election Hilda mounted a failed campaign to run against him, signs that there was bad blood in the family over the matter. Certainly, in 1970, Des was not going to be part of the Haughey-Blaney faction.

Kevin Boland was replaced by Joe Brennan, a party loyalist, from Donegal who could be counted on to keep Blaney in check and ensure Donegal had a presence at the cabinet table. Jim Gibbons filled Blaney's portfolio in Agriculture. George Colley was elevated to the position of Minister for Finance. In this sense, Colley's triumph over his old rival Haughey was for now complete, and for the foreseeable future.

Haughey, limpet-like, clung on to his membership of Fianna Fáil while Boland and Blaney, within two years of the Arms Trial, were out of the party. Boland went off to set up his own party, which went nowhere. Blaney was eventually removed from the party 'for conduct unbecoming for a member of the organisation'. It was to do with his Donegal party machine separately organising their own national collection, the traditional annual party fundraising at church gates. Des O'Malley, many years later, was to be removed from Fianna Fáil under the same disciplinary heading and with a touch of humour gave his own work of memoir the title *Conduct Unbecoming*. Haughey's supporters made the point, in the light of subsequent events in Fianna Fáil, that Haughey stayed loyal to the party even ignominiously voting confidence in Minister Jim Gibbons in a Dáil vote that occurred shortly in the aftermath of being acquitted in the Arms Trial. This was hard stuff to stomach from Haughey's perspective since Gibbons had been the main state or prosecution witness against him. Haughey was prepared to eat humble pie for a number of years. He hunkered down, initially made a few speeches on the north, but as the months turned into years maintained a mantis-like silence about the north and the arms trial.

Meanwhile, the faction around Jack Lynch were not shy in the aftermath of the Arms Trial. The first big test for Lynch was the 1971 Fianna Fáil Ard Fhéis. Feelings were running high. Blaney and Boland were trying to rouse delegates and motions in advance of the date. There was open warfare between delegates in the RDS main hall, in Dublin's Ballsbridge. At one stage, amid the clamour, Dr Patrick Hillery the then Foreign Minister proved his credentials when he grabbed the microphone to declare: "You can have Neil Blaney, You can have Kevin Boland but you cannot have Fianna Fáil." This facing down of the insurrection, at an organisation level, was to continue. According to Blaney's biographer Kevin Rafter by the time the Ard Fhéis came up in 1972, "the Lynch faction was now dominant and totally in control. Throughout the country dissident members had been rooted out and, at all levels of the party structure, positions of responsibility were held by Lynch loyalists". The newer ministers, more likely to be loyal to Lynch, were sent to the country to do this difficult and slightly disreputable work. It caused great bitterness when, more republican-minded, members were forced out of the organisation. It left a very bitter taste. Haughey did, nonetheless, become an elected Vice President of the party at the Ard Fhéis but there were five of these positions and it was a fairly safe bet on his part. Still, it showed he still had support amongst party activists.

Haughey, no longer a busy minister, was liberated from the shackles of office and started a country-wide tour. No location, no corner of the country, was too far away for him to attend if it was a meeting of the ordinary membership. Ministers, up to this point in Fianna Fáil, did not dignify the ordinary membership in such a fashion. Yes the party's senior leaders would appear at by-elections, important funerals and key speaking events. Haughey, for his part, craved any invitation from within the organisation. The invites did not come thick and fast in the early period but before long they came in. Traditionally, for a party big wig to be invited to a constituency, the invite had to come through the local deputy. In some cases a TD would step out of line and invite him but more often the invite came from lower down the ranks but from someone who could issue an invite to him to attend. Sometimes he would attend on a whisper basis. In other words he would arrive, with an informal invite as in nothing in writing, and then proceed to speak. There would be an inquest back in party headquarters every time this happened with the leadership demanding to know who had orchestrated the breaching of the informal ordinance to 'Shun Haughey'. I would sometimes hear my father gossiping with fellow TDs over the phone as to who had invited him.

Haughey's tour of the country was an extraordinary effort for its time. A friend, usually someone from the world of business, would act as driver for the evening and convey him to the event. Part of his strategy was not just to water the grassroots of the party but also to build up wider business support for himself and his aims. Local business people were invited to meet with him before he spoke at the Fianna Fáil event. Haughey was targeting people both within the organisation and outside. One of those who would have accompanied him on these occasions was Albert Reynolds. Reynolds had come into Fianna Fáil via the Blaney by-election operations and had played an active part along with other colleagues from Longford. Reynolds was new to Fianna Fáil and fairly typical of the kind of people who were drawn to Haughey. Reynolds had a network all around the country thanks to his successful dancehall business, which made a fortune for him in the 1960s when Irish people were starved when it came to night time entertainment. Reynolds was sympathetic to Haughey, having attended pretty much every day of the Arms Trial in the Four Courts in Dublin. Reynolds was a family man who had built up big connections in the showband era in the entertainment business across Ireland. He then went on to establish a successful pet food business in Longford. In addition to this, Reynolds had diversified into local newspapers owning his own newspaper, the *Longford News*. Reynolds was selected to run in the 1977 general election, displacing the incumbent TD, at a convention in the Temperance Hall in Mullingar. Few around Lynch quite realised that a lot of the people who eventually won seats for the party in that 1977 election were already Haughey's pledged soldiers.

Haughey liked people who were already a success and could bring something extra to his table. Haughey would arrive at these events with a driver and his Jaguar car. The latter, in these years, was a symbol of dignified affluence. Some preferred the Mercedes but Haughey felt the Jaguar cut a greater dash, with its leather seats and inlay.

My father was still in the government, still a friend of Haughey, but felt it safer to keep contact to a minimum. For this reason I have little or no memory of Haughey coming to our family home either in Athlone or Dublin during this time. He came once about 18 months ahead of the decision by Jack Lynch to resign. My father would more often than not make the visit to Kinsealy instead. I remember the first of these rather furtive visits. My father liked evening Mass on a Sunday. He would ask me to come with him. If he was a Minister he would take Mum's car rather than bother the official Garda driver. He did not do this much and was not a good driver anyway. I suspect my father did not want to let his Garda drivers see him make this particular house call. Our two drivers were of course utterly trustworthy but my father did not want to draw attention to himself when going out to Kinsealy. After the Mass, he would tell me, he was going out to see Haughey, but that I wasn't to tell anyone including my Mum. My first impression of these visits was the huge contrast between the lifestyle Haughey enjoyed and the modest provision at our Castleknock home. Abbeville was a very tastefully appointed Gandon mansion. There was a tree lined avenue, antiques and objects d'art, casually located in most of the rooms. There was a feeling of restrained opulence to the place. As you came in the door there was a huge portrait of Haughey himself, or the Squire as the satirical magazine liked to style him. There were bronze sculptures discreetly placed for effect and the odd bust of a noteworthy person. There were horses being groomed in the stableyard to the back of the house. There were oil paintings of hunting and notable stallions here and there on the walls. On occasion Dad would join him for a drink in what was a private bar in the house. This was something of great awe at the time. It looked and felt like a real bar, optics and draught beer on tap. Haughey would occasionally have a whiskey, my father a cognac or gin and tonic. During this period, Haughey largely stayed clear of the jar. The official story was that he was off it permanently, but he still took a quiet one in the company of close friends. My father always said the liquor did not really suit him and he became a bit all over the place when he drank too much. Haughey preferred to drink in private and not, with rare exceptions, when he was out performing his duties. In this latter respect he was not typical of politicians at the time, most of whom, in my experience, could not resist postponing real discussions until they had a drink in their hand. Haughey's persona was rather professional or stiff most of the times that you met him but he had a ready smile when he wanted to.

In 1973 Fianna Fáil lost the election to a Fine Gael-led coalition with Labour. Liam Cosgrave became Taoiseach and Haughey's long time critic Conor Cruise O'Brien became Minister for Post and Telegraphs. Haughey pulled in a good vote for himself in his constituency where he had battened down the hatches. My father, for his part, lost his seat in Roscommon-Leitrim. He ran for the Senate and Jack Lynch put him into the then-new European Parliament. Membership was by party nomination in those days and the extra money meant a lot to my father who started to resume his practice as a barrister to make ends meet. Haughey's last, old guard, opponent Frank Aiken chose to stand down in the 1973 general election. He was annoyed that Lynch would not block Haughey's nomination as a party candidate. Another obstacle to Haughey's potential return was Erskine Childers. Childers, whom my father had been personal campaigner for at the candidate's own insistence, was elected president in 1973. He was a real thorn in Haughey's side but friendly with my father. My father used to say that Haughey made an enemy of Childers by constantly slagging him at cabinet meetings in the 1960s. Haughey was overly contemptuous of him and Childers returned the complement when Haughey came under pressure in the Arms Trial.

Haughey's constituency machine was an urban mirror image of the operation that Blaney had in Donegal. Haughey attended to his constituents in a way nobody else before or since has done. It cannot have been inexpensive. He was known, for instance, to come to the assistance of distressed families where there might have been difficulty in paying for the funeral of a family member. Funeral expenses have never come cheap in Ireland. Haughey's old friends the Staffords were the undertakers of choice. The Staffords were a very active family in the party. Old Tom Stafford was a charming man with John, his son, subsequently becoming a City Councillor. Apart from burying the Haughey constituents they kept an eye out for him in the North Inner City where their business was based. In addition to this, right up to the point where he finally left the Dáil, Haughey ran a Christmas turkey run for constituents who, again, may have been in distress. This started as an operation targeted at the genuinely needy, but, over time, according to friends of mine who helped with the distribution, it grew and grew. People got to hear of it and asked that their name be put down on the list for the turkey, irrespective of whether it was needed or not. Haughey, like many other politicians, had come up with a good idea that was gradually taken for granted with people treating it as an entitlement of kind. Between the turkeys and the funeral fees, Haughey's constituency operation involved a much higher overhead operation than any other constituency operation in the state. As we now know from the amounts of money he was receiving and the debts he had incurred, Haughey spent a lifetime in politics, both in political and personal terms, just keeping ahead of the incoming bills. Paul McKay, an accountant, who subsequently became involved with the Progressive Democrats, was removed as Fianna Fáil Constituency Party Treasurer when he started asking questions or looking for further information on the constituency accounts.

Haughey, in this time, ran a huge gymkhana, or horse-jumping event, at Kinsealy where he would charge people to come and the proceeds went to the Central Remedial Clinic, a large medical charity based on Dublin's north side. It was a huge success as an event and ran every year in the summer. People crowded to it, mainly it would seem, people who were anxious to get a peek at Haughey's home in Kinsealy. He erected a large marquee where people got fed. Lady Valerie Goulding, the founder of the CRC, was a friend of Haughey's and hugely appreciative of his support. It was quite an event in the social calendar and patronised by well-connected people from the world of business. My parents often went to it in the company of business friends. Haughey still had credibility amongst business and economic decision makers and those among the rich who liked to indulge themselves in the world of horses.

In 1975 Haughey was brought back onto the Fianna Fáil front bench in the Dáil. His responsibility was for Health, something that kept him well away from the mainstream economic policy development of the party. Many had grave reservations about allowing him back, including Des O'Malley who conveyed as much to Lynch. The feeling was that it was better to have him in the tent rather than outside. My father had pushed Lynch to include him. My father always felt it was better to include people and he recognised that despite the misgivings of others Haughey now had a much more significant support base within the party and within the country. Those that had not left or been expelled and were republican minded gravitated to Haughey. They were an important part of the party's broader support base. If the party wanted to win the upcoming election and consolidate their vote in Dublin then Haughey, my father reasoned, had to be on side.

Jack Lynch brought in a very young Séamus Brennan to professionalise the party operation as party General Secretary. Brennan had been sent to the US to study campaigning methods there and came back with some good, new, tactics apart from the many he generated that were his own. Frank Dunlop was appointed as the party's press officer and was far more adept and slick in his approach than those that had come before him. Martin O'Donoghue, a Trinity College Dublin Economist, was brought in to design economic policy under Lynch. O'Donoghue became the author and creator of the by now infamous Big 'Giveaway' manifesto of the 1977 campaign. In fairness to Haughey, he did not agree with the thrust of the manifesto, nor indeed did my father. My father's view was that politically the Cosgrave coalition were unpopular enough as things stood and that Lynch was still a significant electoral asset. Haughey had reservations about the economic sustainability of the plan. In the event, Haughey was in no position to object given that he was still in a position of isolation within the party's senior ranks. Haughey and my father chose to silently absent themselves from the launch of the 1977 manifesto. Since neither were part of the tight, inner group, around Lynch they were not missed on this occasion. Few expected that the giveaway manifesto would contribute to a Fianna Fáil electoral landslide.

Haughey, though on the frontbench, was a lot lower profile in terms of media presence. The party hierarchy was not putting him out there as part of their official plans. Haughey was simply tolerated but certainly not considered a friend to anyone in the ruling elite of the party. My father on the other hand had been a frequent media presence since the party had lost office in 1973. He began to develop a reputation as the person the party put on television when they had problems, as a kind of defender of things that were difficult to defend. One of the most important things, in order to get the Fianna Fáil vote out in Dublin city, was to ensure that Haughey was seen visibly to be part of the team. Some in the city still grumbled that Haughey was being left out and of course rumours abounded that he himself was not committed to the cause. My father orchestrated a seemingly spontaneous photo opportunity whereby Haughey and Lynch, both campaigning in the area, would simply run into each other by arrangement at Phibsboro Shopping Centre, just north of the city centre. The picture of the two together sent a strong message to Dublin supporters that the party was a unified team. The extent to which this had to be arranged and orchestrated surreptitiously underlined the extent of Haughey's isolation and the distrust the Lynch faction had for him.

Election night in 1977 was an extraordinary thing. In my father's constituency we went back to the West County Hotel in Chapelizod to observe the televised coverage. All of the party's key figures were topping the poll with ludicrously high votes, Lynch, Haughey and my father too. There were several thousand people in the hotel and the whole place erupted with this enormous roar when the screen confirmed, followed by the announcer confirming, that Conor Cruise O'Brien had lost his seat. O'Brien was no fan of Fianna Fáil, nor indeed of Charlie Haughey. O'Brien, now unceremoniously ejected from the Dáil by the electorate, would soon turn his hand to journalism, writing columns for the *Irish Times*, then later again for the *Irish Independent*. He was to become the Bete Noir to Haughey and everything he represented. The main target for Cruise O'Brien's ire both within government and outside it was Irish republicanism. Haughey with his Arms Trial connections to the Provisional IRA was persona *non grata* in his eyes too.

CHAPTER EIGHT

THE HEAVE

Haughey was appointed Minister for Health and Social Welfare in the new Lynch government of 1977. My father, a little annoyed given his loyalty to Lynch over the previous few years, was made Minister for Fisheries. He had given his all to keep the party together under Lynch but was clearly not part of the inner group that was running things. In 1973 he had been Minister for Foreign Affairs, so the appointment to Fisheries represented a significant setback. George Colley approached my father and sympathised, stating that he did not agree with what was done. According to my father, Colley appeared genuinely shocked. My father was under no illusion about it. Colley was part of the inner group around Lynch. My father thought his talents were regarded but apparently not so. My father hid his disappointment and got on with his job. The big majority and the new deputies were to turn out to be a bit of a nightmare for Jack Lynch. The new deputies were more boisterous than any other group seen before this. They also contained a strong cohort of both Haughey supporters as well as those from the deeper, more republican side of the party. Neither of these two groups were much enamoured with Jack Lynch.

Haughey's time in Health and Social Welfare was not wasted. Previously, ministers would help their own deputies when they wanted to bring a delegation to see the Minister. However, ministers traditionally did not go overboard on pleasing their own backbenchers on constituency matters. Haughey took his obligations to fellow TDs to another level. Haughey put forward a service level for TDs that was second to none. His office team was wired to look after them. Many of these new TDs and others were impressed. Haughey had a reputation quickly established amongst TDs that he could get things done for them. In terms of his ministerial portfolio, Haughey went for initiatives that generated positive publicity for the department and himself. One such initiative had the appearance of gimmick but certainly got him noticed by the mothers of Ireland. He issued a free toothbrush to every young child in the country ostensibly to brush up the country's efforts in the area of oral hygiene. The Public Health side of things was boosted with other campaigns around fitness and not smoking. Much to the chagrin of his cabinet colleagues who smoked, he banned smoking from the platform of the Fianna Fáil Ard Fhéis. To his credit, he was one of the first ministers in Europe to restrain and legislate against tobacco advertising, something this global industry did not appreciate. The Irish regulations from this time were often held up internationally as a template for others to follow. An English friend of mine who was paid by the tobacco industry to lobby used to complain loudly about the way Ireland had set itself against his industry and its repercussions at an EU level.

Elsewhere, things were not going well for the government itself. The giveaway election manifesto had got rid of car tax and rates on houses. The exchequer deficit was climbing and the national debt ballooned, increasing by £2 billion within the two short years that Fianna Fáil had been office. Lynch had put the Economist, now TD, Martin O'Donoghue in a huge new ministry called the Department of Economic Planning that was committed to pump-priming the economy. Despite falls in unemployment, the numbers out of work still remained high. PAYE workers started taking to the streets over punitive rates of taxation. About one million people took to the streets in protest. Ironically, the cause of this protest movement was not just punitive rates of tax on PAYE workers but a levy designed to ensure that farmers paid their own fair share of the taxation burden. The speed with which the levy against farmer's income was modified by pressure from rural deputies and the Minister for Agriculture enraged urban workers. Then, to compound the difficulties facing the government, a prolonged post office strike took place which nobody in government appeared prepared or skilled enough to solve. Haughey offered to help and his government colleagues allowed him to do so.

Haughey had developed strong connections to the trade unions during his wilderness years and in particular to its head, Michael Mullin. Haughey told his ministerial colleagues he had been having private talks with the trade union leaders. It was now the first half of 1979 and the strike had dragged on. The cost to the exchequer if the government caved in to the demands would have been enormous in terms of knock on claims in the wider public sector. The authors of *The Boss* Joe Joyce and Peter Murtagh take up the story:

> *"Other ministers were content to have Haughey do this for a time, but then they became suspicious that he was trying to prolong the strike in anticipation of the damage it would cause to Lynch's leadership."[39]*

A friend of mine who was involved in the dispute says the strikers in one location in Dublin city centre were delighted with Haughey. There was this big sorting office near Haughey's office. Haughey would send money down to a

[39]Joyce, Joe and Murtagh, Peter, *The Boss – Charles J. Haughey in Government*, Poolbeg Press, 1983

local publican to ensure the men got sandwiches and soup while they manned the picket line in very cold weather. Some see it as an act of kindness, some of his colleagues see it as him undermining his own government. At the very least of it Haughey could be seen to have been keeping all of his options open. The oil crisis of 1979 dealt another body blow to Jack Lynch's high spending government. Oil prices soared internationally as a result of the toppling of the Shah of Iran by Islamic revolutionaries. At home in Ireland the public were treated to long queues at petrol stations, higher prices and a shortage of supply. It gave an additional element of instability to an economy that was already faltering.

Haughey, during his term as Minister, brought forward a modest reform of the country's legal prohibition of the use of condoms. It allowed for greater access but restricted the availability to bona fide married couples or people with a prescription. The Catholic Church was still quite powerful. Religious zealots denounced the measure, liberals felt it was a step forward but the media derided it in comical terms. The measure itself was described as 'An Irish solution to an Irish problem'. Jim Gibbons, a virulent opponent of Haughey, and now Minister for Agriculture did not show up to vote for the legislation. Gibbons was a devout Catholic but people concluded, because there was no sanction applied to him for not voting for the government, that there was one rule for those around Lynch and another rule for everyone else. Gibbons stayed in the government and was not even the subject of private disciplinary measures. The tongues were sent wagging in Fianna Fáil with many assuming that Gibbons, because of his decision to give evidence in the Arms Trial, had some form of leverage over Lynch so that he could not in effect sack him. My father, a friend of Gibbons when in the European Parliament with him, always assumed that the Lynch team had got to Gibbons in relation to his evidence at the Arms Trial. However it now appeared that Gibbons had got to them. Lynch's authority as Taoiseach was about to come apart.

In September 1979 Pope John Paul II came on a visit to Ireland. The whole country went wild. Over a million people gathered in Dublin's Phoenix Park for an open air mass. The prelude to this event saw hundreds of journalists descending on Dublin ahead of the event. With little to report, a series of rumours went into circulation that a scandal was about to embroil the President, Dr Patrick Hillery, about alleged marital infidelity. The story was apparently going to be carried in a British tabloid. The President eventually quelled the whole matter by simply stating he was not resigning as some of the rumours seemed to be hinting at. It was all a bit fevered, but in later years Hillery was to suggest that the rumours had been generated by people close to Haughey in his bid to replace Jack Lynch. It was a bizarre moment in Irish life. It is hard to imagine how Haughey would have benefitted from destabilising the non-political office of the President. In any event, the Papal visit went ahead undisturbed by the rumours. Up in the old Papal Nuncio building after the big, open air mass, in the park, I spent the rest of the day having Irish coffees with Bobby Molloy and other members of the government who had shown up for the drinks afterwards. My father had brought me along. Few, if anybody, could have guessed at that moment that we were now in a countdown to Jack Lynch's departure as Taoiseach. Prior to the Pope's visit, Charles Haughey had come to visit my father in our home in Castleknock. He had driven himself in the familiar Jaguar. The two retired to the kitchen. He was seeking advice on what he should do.

The summer had seen the Fianna Fáil party trounced in the European elections of 1979 with support dropping to 34.6% from the high of 50.6% two years earlier. It was the worst result the party had got since it had been founded. There was very little room for papering over the cracks on a result like that. There had also been huge public embarrassment for the government because of the murder of Earl Mountbatten on his yacht off Mullaghmore in County Sligo. The Earl and his family spent their summers in Ireland. In August, the boat was blown sky high from the water by a massive, radio-controlled, bomb placed there by the IRA. Mountbatten, a member of the British Royal family, was a favourite uncle to the current heir to the British throne Prince Charles. It was an atrocious attack and left very raw feeling in Britain towards the Irish. To the outside world and to those within Ireland it looked like the Lynch government had lost its grip in terms of the security situation in the country. My father, one of the few ministers in the country at the time, travelled up to meet with the survivors of the blast and relations of Mountbatten. He was there on behalf of the government. He was struck by how courteous and friendly they were to him given the appalling nature of what had happened. Some of the survivors were in bad shape but they insisted on stating to my father that it had not and would not change their attitude to Ireland. North of the border on the same day, the IRA ambushed and killed 18 British Paratroop Regiment soldiers at Warrenpoint. There was huge pressure on Jack Lynch's government to tighten up security co-operation with the British along the border counties. Jack Lynch, as Taoiseach, attended the Mountbatten funeral. Afterwards he and George Colley attended a meeting with the new British Prime Minister Margaret Thatcher. It was tense and difficult. At home in Ireland it was perceived that Lynch had allowed himself to be browbeaten by her. He came across as weak in his dealings with the British. The public impression was created that in a fashion Lynch had been summoned to Mrs Thatcher's residence and as she was famous for doing, been 'handbagged'.

The fact that Lynch had appeared for the meeting, still in mourning suit, only added to this impression.

Meanwhile, a group of five deputies had formed themselves into an informal caucus to secure a change in the direction of Fianna Fáil. These, the so-called 'Gang of Five' included Albert Reynolds, Seán Doherty, Tom McEllistrim, Jackie Fahey and Mark Killilea. There were others outside of this group who were equally determined to remove Lynch and replace him with Haughey. Others like Charlie McCreevy, Paddy Power, and Seán Calleary were also keen to secure change. Pádraig Flynn was also involved. Many of these TDs conducted their intrigues in the old Jury's Hotel in Ballsbridge where a lot of Fianna Fáil backbenchers stayed while in Dublin for the Dáil sittings. It was not long before these informal gatherings turned into active plotting, with meetings going on in TDs offices in Leinster House. Few if anybody could link these TDs to Haughey. There were no formal signs that they were even in contact with him. It was a classic destabilisation campaign with the target, Jack Lynch, blissfully unaware of how its was being co-ordinated and how determined it was.

Síle de Valera, elected in the landslide of 1977 for South Dublin, was first out with a highly critical speech in relation to the drift in Northern Ireland policy under Lynch. This was given at a traditional commemoration event in Fermoy and got all the more attention because she was a grand daughter of the party's founder. Haughey himself was keeping silent throughout this big push. In quick succession Tom McEllistrim of Kerry made a critical attack on the British military over flights from the North. Bad luck struck for Lynch when the party lost two by-elections in his native Cork in November of 1979. Dr Bill Loughnane, a charismatic backbencher, and fiddle player from Clare was next to speak out, virtually accusing Jack Lynch of lying over the extent of our state's security co-operation with the British. Lynch was abroad at the time and it is always taken badly when any deputy, your own or others, criticises the head of government when they are abroad representing the country. Lynch requested from the U.S. that Loughnane be expelled from the parliamentary party. The task fell to George Colley. Colley chaired the meeting in Lynch's absence and managed to further alienate deputies. According to my father, he created more enemies than friends on the issue. In the end the leadership group around Colley had to accept that Loughnane would withdraw his comment. It was a humiliating climb-down and it led to a spate of petitions, including one, which gathered 20 names asking for the leadership issue to be addressed in the party. This was a backbench revolt like no other. Lynch decided to issue his resignation on the 5th of December 1979. My father had advised him he could have faced down the pressure from the backbenchers but my father formed the view that the fight was out of him and that he was tired. Afterwards, he vehemently denied he was pushed, insisting that his intention was to retire in January of 1980. One of the reasons he left early was because George Colley had told him he had the numbers to win a leadership contest.

The leadership contest to replace him was set for 7th December, just two days after Lynch issued his resignation. Colley, O'Malley and Martin O'Donoghue had made a serious miscalculation. They reckoned foolishly that a short contest would suit Colley. The government, but especially those around Lynch, was seriously out of touch with backbench opinion. The atmosphere became frenzied around Leinster House. My father declared early on that he would not be offering a view on how he was voting. His private reasoning was that it was going to be a tight contest and he wanted to be neutral so that he could serve whichever leader emerged from the contest. Behind the scenes he was advising Haughey via the telephone from our home in Castleknock. Colley's campaign team included Gerry Collins. They were sifting through the TDs making assumptions that were not always correct. It became a contest between the incumbent government and the backbenches. Colley was not in a position to offer jobs in the government whereas Haughey, leading a backbench revolt, was able to offer key supporters all sorts of things. While Colley's campaigners bolstered their colleagues in government so that nobody declared for Haughey, the Haughey campaign was picking up wavering backbench support. Haughey begged my father to come out and openly declare for him. My father declined but advised him on a number of members of the government that might be amenable to do so. He also steered him in the direction of his friends in the parliamentary party that might also be prepared to support.

It is indicative of the naiveté of George Colley that right up to the eve of the actual vote he was convinced that Ray MacSharry was going to vote for him. MacSharry was a Junior Minister in Finance with Colley but was one of the major and known drivers of the Haughey campaign. My father thought this hilarious. One night during the campaign he came home after a few drinks and we badgered him about who was going to win.

He said it would be a tight vote, probably Haughey, but it was too close to call. When we asked him who he was voting for he complained he was faced with the choice of voting for a 'Knave or a Fool'. It was so close that my father got together with Ray Burke, who was voting for Colley, and they each decided to mark their ballot paper in the same way so that no matter who had won they could claim they had voted for the winner if challenged on the matter by pointing out the distinct mark they had left on the ballot paper. My father voted for Haughey and Ray voted for Colley. The idea of the marking was to insulate Burke against a Haughey victory and my father against a victory by Colley. Haughey beat Colley by 44 votes to 38.

On the eve of the vote Michael O'Kennedy, a lifelong friend of my fathers, went into the Colley campaign office and informed them that he was voting for Haughey.

It was a huge bombshell for them at this stage. Some of the Colley team followed him out of the office and pinned him up against a wall. He was called a rat and told he could not do this. It has always been claimed that it was Haughey's canvas team who were applying the strong-arm tactics. Colley's team was capable of the same approach. O'Kennedy's decision was probably motivated by what he saw as the need to change the party's whole approach to the North. He was quite republican and had been criticised by the Lynch faction, of which he was part, for changing the party policy from Unity by Consent to one of favouring a British Declaration of Intent to Withdraw. However he had worked carefully on this policy change and had been not thanked for the effort he had put in while in opposition. He was subsequently appointed Minister for Finance and European Commissioner. Interestingly, when Haughey was Minister for Health he was taken into the Mater Hospital for an operation. At the time, Haughey was still very much a pariah amongst his colleagues. Despite the fact that all of his colleagues knew he was ill, only two, Michael O'Kennedy and my father, bothered to visit him while there. Few of the Lynch faction had shown such consideration for Haughey.

Haughey, after the ritual press conference and acknowledgement of victory, retreated to his office quarters to celebrate with his closest supporters. My father cleared away from the premises on the basis that there would be quite a few sore heads around. Haughey prepared to form his first cabinet on becoming Taoiseach. His enthusiastic backbenchers filled Haughey's head with suggestions as to who had voted for him. Some were suggesting my father had not voted for him. My father did not appear to be too perturbed about these reports he was receiving from inside Haughey's entourage. Haughey was on the phone to him fairly promptly after victory, seeking advice, on whom he should trust and what he should do. Haughey had a lot of supporters to assuage. In staging his challenge he had not been too fussy on whom he picked up on the way along. They would now be asking him for their reward.

Haughey's slow climb back from the abyss of the Arms Trial had been both dramatic and to a certain extent thrilling. There were a lot of expectations riding on him, not least amongst those virulent backbenchers who had staked out the ground for him and hastened Jack Lynch's retreat. The crowd around Lynch were a bit shell-shocked. Their world had collapsed around them, their nemesis was now in charge. Apart from his diligent attention to the grassroots, his cultivation of the backbenches, what had brought Haughey to this point was his steadfast ambition. Added to this, alone amongst Irish politicians, he had not neglected the sphere of public policy. In his wilderness years he had become an advocate for the arts, heritage and even in the area of conservation. Apart from his well-established views on the north of Ireland he was seen as a man who had a businesslike approach to running the country. Mrs Thatcher had come to power across the water within the Tory party, as a result of a similar revolt against the softer politics of Edward Heath. Haughey was in an ideal position to change the country and the economic vision of the government. The 1977 manifesto and the indolence of those around Lynch had let the economy slip into a mess. Haughey might have been a lot of things but he certainly was not lazy.

Haughey now had a new leader of Fine Gael to contend with. Liam Cosgrave had left the position in the wake of the 1977 electoral defeat. Cosgrave belonged to the old school. Garret FitzGerald, though he had, through his father, a connection to the old Free State, was one of the group from the 1960s onwards who were positioned on the liberal wing of the party. They had tried to stake out Cosgrave with regard to special powers legislation that would have given draconian powers to crack down on the

IRA. Cosgrave was in danger of seeing his party desert him on the measure and thus faced embarrassment as he belonged to the conservative, law and order, wing of the party. A bomb, believed to have been the work of loyalist paramilitaries, was detonated in central Dublin on the eve of the vital vote. His party rallied to him and voted for the measure. Later Cosgrave made a triumphant statement at his party's 1972 Ard Fheis declaring there was no more room for 'mongrel foxes' in Fine Gael, a veiled reference to FitzGerald and others who were opposing him. Cosgrave was a keen horseman and frequently rode in the hunt.

FitzGerald chose the moment of Haughey's nomination for the position to make his famous 'Flawed Pedigree' speech quoted in chapter one of this book. The speech was a blatant effort to surface all of the doubts that already existed about Haughey given the many controversies in his career; the Arms Trial, the money and his sheer ambition. Given the closeness of the Fianna Fáil leadership contest it was also a pitch or appeal to the disillusioned deputies who had backed Colley. It was also an attempt to seek support in the wider country from people who might have voted but also had reservations about Haughey. "I must speak not only for the Opposition but for many in Fianna Fáil who may not be free to say what they believe or to express their deep fears for the future of this country under the proposed leadership, people who are not free to reveal what they know and what led them to oppose this man with a commitment far beyond the normal," said Fitzgerald. The ferocity of this speech left a bad taste amongst his listeners. I was there that day and it was hard not to feel pity for Haughey's mother, family and friends as they listened to it in the public viewing gallery in the Dáil. The speech by the conventional wisdom of the time may have back-fired on FitzGerald and in fact created sympathy for Haughey. Haughey sat motionless in his chair with that impassive, icy, look that he would take on when facing ferocious criticism. He told his colleagues to exercise restraint and not respond to the provocation. Haughey also insisted on sitting through the whole debate on his own, dissuading colleagues to sit with him in moral support.

Garret FitzGerald was to prove to be a formidable, agile and very intellectual opponent for Haughey. The speech set out the scene whereby he would make Haughey, himself, the issue in Irish politics. It was a bold gambit and one which was to achieve some resonance within the country. At another level the speech gave psychological sustenance to those within the Fianna Fáil party who wished to continue and disrupt Haughey's leadership. The speech in many ways de-legitimised Haughey and his arrival to power.

CHAPTER NINE

TAOISEACH

In the aftermath of a shocking defeat, the clique of people who had gathered around Jack Lynch as leader were now feeling very raw. They had been in power for so long that they had acquired a sense of entitlement. They saw many of the people who supported the political heave against them as unsuitable people, unsuitable for public or executive office. They were also more than a little put out about the manner in which the famous Gang of Five had taken matters in the party into their own hands.

They knew that Haughey was behind these men but could not make a direct connection. Soon, the investigative journalist Vincent Browne and his *Magill* magazine gave them an insight into who these men were and how the whole thing had been organised. It is clear from the series of articles that the pro-Haughey backbench revolt had been anything but spontaneous. The articles may also have added to the bitterness surrounding the tight leadership vote. It had the look and feel of an organised conspiracy.

My father's advice to Haughey in the immediate aftermath of his election as Taoiseach was to 'heal the wounds' created by the leadership contest. It was my father's instinct to mollify rather than rub your opponents' nose in it when they had lost. In the days after the leadership contest,

Haughey's supporters were pouring over the voting records and cross checking their lists to establish who exactly had voted for him. There was still an air of triumphalism about Haughey's roughneck supporters, some of them, in fact, suspecting that my father had not voted for Haughey. These enthusiastic members of the fabled back bench revolt felt entitled to see a clean sweep in the ministerial ranks. Everyone was jockeying for position. Gene FitzGerald, the Lynch cabinet member, was one of the first to take his courage in his hands and pledge loyalty to the new Boss. He arrived in Haughey's office with a bottle of whiskey. Gene, like Lynch, was from Cork but he was not going down with the Lynch ship. He was the first of the previous Lynch cabinet to extend the hand of peace.

Haughey, in selecting his cabinet, was sensitive to the situation he found himself in and the divided party he now presided over. His tight margin of victory meant he would have to retain a great many of those from the Lynch cabinet who had not voted for him. Haughey's nemesis from the Arms Trial, Jim Gibbons, was dropped along with long-term Colley supporter Bobby Molloy and of course the Minister for Economic Planning Martin O'Donoghue. Haughey blamed O'Donoghue and his foolish spending policies for the difficulties in the economy. He not only dropped O'Donoghue but also dismantled and abolished his ministry. Thousands of additional civil servants had been hired under the O'Donoghue fiscal expansion plan. At a loss as to where to put O'Donoghue's officials, a good many of them were brought into a greatly enlarged Department of the Taoiseach. Thus began a new era of centrally driven government. From that time onwards the Taoiseach and Taoiseach's Department would act more like an Executive Presidency rather than the previous cabinet government system. Because the Taoiseach's department now had additional civil servants, a system was developed whereby units within the department became responsible for coordinating with key line departments. From then on, there was a day to day scrutiny of line departments directly from the Taoiseach's office. It helped to speed up decision making and clear issues before they reached the cabinet for actual discussion. However, for individual ministers, it meant the department of the Taoiseach was now reaching into individual departments in a much more intrusive fashion than before.

Five significant Haughey allies were brought into cabinet: Ray MacSharry, Albert Reynolds, the first female appointment to cabinet since Countess Markievicz – Máire Geoghegan-Quinn, Paddy Power and Michael Woods. The balance of the Gang of Five group was accommodated along with other key Haughey loyalists amongst the ranks of Ministers of State. Haughey, because of the promises he had made, now expanded the actual numbers of junior ministers to accommodate his supporters, a measure that was accompanied by much cynicism. Michael O'Kennedy, the only cabinet member who had openly supported him, became Minister for Finance. My father received the upgrade he certainly felt he deserved, to the role of Minister for Foreign Affairs, a position he had held prior to the 1973 election.

Colley, though retaining his title as Tánaiste, was given the lesser portfolio of Energy, though he had been offered and refused Foreign Affairs. The anger over what had happened to Lynch and his loss in the leadership contest still clearly rankled with him. He was a sore, very sore loser. Haughey said in the immediate aftermath of his election as leader that Colley had indicated he would give him full support. But Colley issued a statement to the effect that his loyalty to Haughey was only as Taoiseach and not in effect as party leader. This offer of conditional loyalty, he claimed, was appropriate given what had been done to Jack Lynch. As Bruce Arnold notes, "It was an extraordinary outburst and represented immediate grounds for Colley's dismissal from the Government, and his expulsion from the party".[40] In fact, Colley had told Haughey he was going to make the statement. It was a surprising and damaging sign of weakness on Haughey's part that he allowed Colley to go ahead with the speech. Privately, behind the scenes, Colley had told Bruce Arnold that the Lynch faction were committed to staying together and getting rid of Haughey as quickly as possible. Haughey really had missed a golden opportunity to make an example of Colley. My father depicted Colley's actions as 'sour grapes' and, like Haughey, underestimated the extent to which the Colley-O'Malley faction would disrupt things in the future. My father was a little surprised that Haughey did not take the opportunity to move Colley on.

On the 9th of January 1980, Haughey took the opportunity to give a state of the nation address, live on television, in an effort to condition people to a period of retrenchment in the public finances. It was a brave move on his part, correctly identifying the need to put the economy right. It was, in a sense, what people were waiting to hear. People, at that point, saw Haughey as the perfect antidote to the reckless spending initiatives undertaken by the Jack Lynch government under the direction of Professor Martin O'Donoghue as Minister for Economic Planning. Haughey was playing to his own strengths as an accountant who wanted to balance the books, and a person perceived to be strong on business matters. His TV address struck a chord with commentators and the public alike. He stated blandly, "as a community we are living away beyond our means". What followed was an exercise to demonstrate how the figures, behind the exchequer, simply did not add up and that as a nation, "We have been borrowing enormous amounts of money, borrowing at a rate which just cannot continue". He spoke about lost days through stoppages, strikes, industrial unrest, an appeal for wage restraint and the prospect of major spending cuts. However, what

---

[40]Arnold, Bruce, *Haughey – His Life and Unlucky Deeds*, Harper Collins, 1993, p. 161

happened next was quite the opposite to what was being recommended in the address. Haughey seems to have backed off and his cabinet colleagues, some of whom were still wedded to the O'Donoghue economic expansion model, were strongly resisting the medicine he wanted to administer.

"He very quickly took fright. In fact he abandoned the 9 January strategy for Ireland's economy. And when the budget was delivered at the end of that month, it was full of compromises. An innately generous streak in Haughey won through and he produced a number of popular provisions among them almost prodigal taxation changes designed to win support from the PAYE sector, a favourable change in married couples' taxation law and a generous, across-the-board 25 per cent increase in social welfare. It was a blatant reversal of the January statement."[41]

The Fianna Fáil Ard Fhéis in February was to see him reiterate the phrase that the country was living beyond its means.

The 1980 Fianna Fáil Ard Fhéis was an extraordinary affair. Held in the RDS, Ballsbridge, there were queues of people filling into the main hall in the early morning before anything substantial had got underway. There was a sense of anticipation and energy in the venue. A new group of people were striding around the hall. There were, naturally enough, markedly more Dublin people at the event. Owing to all of the expulsions in the aftermath of the Arms Trial, there was now a flood of people coming back into the party. Haughey's supporters traditionally occupied the left hand side of the audience in the Lynch years. On this occasion they were everywhere. Before Haughey's evening speech there was hardly any room to move. Some people were fainting from the heat and in the environs of the RDS there were people swarming around in the hopes

[41]Arnold, Bruce, *Haughey – His Life and Unlucky Deeds*, Harper Collins, 1993, p. 165

of getting a ticket. It was a huge homecoming event for the republican element in the party and they were about to show their appreciation for Haughey. Haughey's speech covered the usual subjects but the audience really only got going when he mentioned Northern Ireland. Haughey had declared, on becoming Taoiseach, that his first priority was the ending of partition by agreement. When it came to the North, Haughey's gravelly tones rasped out a phrase that lifted the roof. "Northern Ireland", he intoned, was a "failed entity". He followed up with the words "artificially created, artificially sustained". The roaring, cheers and whistles that accompanied this remark were extraordinary. I was seated somewhere around the middle of the hall and to me it was like a Baptist revival meeting not a political conference. There were placard-wielding party members at the front and sides of the hall, holding up pictures of Charlie like he was a religious icon. What I thought to be a mild-mannered Tipperary man sitting beside me suddenly became transformed into a red-faced fanatic shouting out loudly, "Give it the timber Charlie, Give it the timber".

Despite the somewhat menacing rhetoric, Haughey was cast out on a much more moderate path. His argument was that because of the failure of the six county state, an internal solution was pointless, and now he proposed meeting with the British Prime Minister to bring about a diplomatic solution which would be brokered by Dublin and London working together. In May of 1980, some months after the Ard Fhéis, he met with British Prime Minister Margaret Thatcher at Downing Street. Haughey put a lot of energy into this meeting, boosting up its importance, fussing over the final details and was clearly out to impress upon Thatcher that he was a man with whom she could do business. He brought an expensive gift of a Georgian teapot made of Irish silver. There was also reference to a present of a pair of Irish wolfhounds, the latter gift a historical reference to Grace O'Malley, the Irish pirate Queen's visit to Elizabeth I at Hampton Court where a similar gift had been given. The symbolism of his visit was not lost on Haughey. There was a cordial, rather than confrontational, feeling to the meeting at Downing Street. A Tory friend of mine, from my time as a journalist covering Thatcher at the House of Commons, told me that British officials were impressed with Haughey, who apparently was the first person ever to compliment Mrs Thatcher on her legs. Haughey's toughness and intellect were similar to hers and in her subsequent memoirs Mrs Thatcher professed to preferring Haughey to Lynch, despite the ups and downs in the subsequent political relationship. Thatcher was a staunch supporter of the union but Haughey drew the conclusion, as did my father, that the British establishment were committed to making some effort towards a solution of the Irish issue. This was a getting to know you meeting and the portents were good. The Whitehall Mandarin civil servant Lord Powell was later to remark that there was a 'glint' in Haughey's eyes that Mrs Thatcher had found attractive.[42] In the meantime, officials began to prepare for a more substantial meeting that was to take place between them later on that year, the venue Dublin.

In 1980 my brother Brian had invited me into Bewley's Café, on Grafton Street, to meet with a visiting journalist called McDermott from Derry. The man's nickname was 'Wombat'. He wrote for the *Derry Journal* and was somehow related to one of the other students who joined us for coffee that morning in Bewley's. He had silver-rimmed glasses and a reddish complexion. The excitement around the meeting was that 'Wombat' was well-connected in republican circles and would have something to say. His family members had served sentences in the notorious Long Kesh Prison (HM Prison Maze) in the north. What he told us was both surprising and to us a revelation. He predicted that Mrs Thatcher would be the greatest boost for Irish nationalism in a generation. Those of us around the table, who were

---

[42]Quoted from Dr Stephen Kelly, Lecturer in Modern History, Liverpool Hope University, in an article written in the *Irish Times*, December 24th, 2014

left wing like myself, were more than a little puzzled. He went on to explain that being an English nationalist she would resist, strongly, the republican movement and that her robustness in dealing with it would drive more people into it. He developed a scenario around the Dirty Protest, which was ongoing in the Maze Prison at the time and predicted that this would escalate to a full-scale hunger strike because of Mrs Thatcher's intransigence and the British authorities' refusal to accord political status to the prisoners. I am astounded to this day at the talk this man gave. Pretty much every one of his predictions that morning was subsequently borne out. Later on, as events in the Maze unfolded, my friends and I would use our spare periods from school to go down to O'Connell Street and lend a hand to the permanent hunger strike protest that was going on there. To me it seemed unjust that the British government was treating the prisoners as they were. It was not so unreasonable that prisoners would be allowed to wear their own clothing rather than that allocated to them by the British prison authorities. That particular privilege had been given in a previous period but then without explanation removed. Special Category Status had differentiated these prisoners from ordinary criminal prisoners. In response, we would stand outside the GPO, or on occasion don black armbands, and discourage people from shopping in the nearby British Home Stores, while handing out leaflets about the hunger strike. I had told my father of my concerns about the Hunger Strike but he seemed to have had other things on his mind.

In November of 1980, during a by-election campaign in Donegal, Síle de Valera had again been outspoken on a republican issue, though this time Charles Haughey was Taoiseach and not Jack Lynch. The tone of the speech was very critical of Mrs Thatcher and the story is taken up by Raymond Smith who was covering the by-election for his newspaper:

"Síle launched into a bitter attack on Mrs. Thatcher's handling of the H-Block issue, accusing her of lack of compassion and recalling that 'not once but twice in the Commons, the British Prime Minister issued callous, unfeeling and self-righteous statements' on the British Government's stance. She concluded by saying that if the situation was allowed to deteriorate further, then the British Government 'must shoulder the responsibility for further deaths, whether it be in H-Block, on the streets or elsewhere throughout the six counties'."[43]

It is indicative of the importance that Haughey placed in his relationship with Mrs Thatcher, at this stage, that Síle de Valera's speech was very strongly denounced by a government spokesman stating that it did not in any way reflect the views of the Irish government. It would seem that in his anxiety to actually build a relationship with Mrs Thatcher, Haughey was prepared to ignore the warning voices coming from inside and outside his party about the potential enormity of the H-Blocks dispute.

My father had attended the London meeting with Mrs Thatcher and was hugely enthusiastic about the follow-on, which was set for 6 December 1980. I had breakfast with him on the morning of the summit and tackled him again on the Maze protest issue. He was non-committal on the matters I raised with him. It was to be a huge British delegation. Dublin Castle, the old seat of British rule in Ireland, was to be the location for the meeting. Extraordinary security precautions were being taken, helicopters, Gardaí and the army everywhere. The British delegation contained some of the most senior officials that had ever visited Ireland, in its long history with Britain. At Ministerial level it included Sir [now Lord] Geoffrey Howe, Chancellor of the Exchequer; Lord Peter Carrington, Foreign Secretary; and Sir Humphrey Atkins, the Northern Ireland Secretary. My

---

[43]Smith, Raymond, *Haughey and O'Malley – The Quest for Power*, Aherlow Publishers, 1986, p. 61

father was particularly proud of the fact that it was he who came up with the phraseology the 'totality of relationships', which became, in effect the way in which Haughey and himself were able to trumpet the significance of the summit itself. They were both accused of having over-hyped the event and added to Unionist anxieties which Mrs Thatcher later set out to assuage. The high level joint studies that were initiated were significant. It was hard to convince the domestic media of the significance of this summit given the vagueness of the communiqué. The efforts by my father and Haughey to talk up the prospects of institutional arrangements and the constitutional position of Northern Ireland seem to be part of a general effort to enhance the value of what was discussed. That said, my father always insisted privately that the British both in the background and publicly were making hugely favourable noises and that the process of joint studies was not in fact limited in its scope. However, Haughey had succeeded at a formal level, at least, to take Anglo-Irish relations to a higher plane, which was one of his objectives when he set out as Taoiseach.

According to Dr Stephen Kelly who has studied the latest British records about the meeting in 1980 that have been released under the 30 year rule: "behind closed doors senior members of the British Civil Service, against Thatcher's wishes, were willing to concede that the Irish government be entitled to play a legitimate role in the affairs of Northern Ireland."[44] Sir Robert Armstrong, of the cabinet office and others on the British side were prepared to give Ireland a functional role in finding a solution to the issue in Northern Ireland. This was an advance of some significance given later rhetorical assertions by Mrs Thatcher that Northern Ireland was as British as Finchley, her London constituency. My father, an astute observer of the British establishment, felt there was greater significance in what the permanent

---

[44]Quoted from Dr Stephen Kelly, Lecturer in Modern History, Liverpool Hope University, in an article written in the *Irish Times*, December 24th, 2014

government members, like Armstrong, were stating rather than what Mrs Thatcher might vocalise in parliament. As T. Ryle Dwyer puts it,

"Margaret Thatcher promptly denied there was any intention of altering the constitutional position of the Six Counties, but Ian Paisley exploited Unionist uneasiness by taking to what he called the 'Carson Trail' in order to demonstrate the intensity of Unionist opposition to constitutional change. A whole series of demonstrations were organised throughout Northern Ireland to rail against the joint studies."[45]

In May of 1981, Bobby Sands, a hunger striker, died, after having being elected an MP to the British parliament. His death brought huge international coverage and sympathy for his cause. It led to a surge in recruitment to the IRA and acted in a way to revive the fortunes of the IRA North of the border, but in particular the newly emergent team leadership of Gerry Adams and Martin McGuinness. The Hunger Strike issue was to become an issue in the south too with two candidates running on that ticket taking seats in the June general election, thus depriving Fianna Fáil of the numbers they needed for re-election to government. The ghoulish circumstances of Sands' death and that of those who followed him only served to undermine public confidence in the process that Haughey had initiated with Mrs Thatcher. The fact that the latter was not prepared to listen to Haughey, or anyone else for that matter, on the issue of the Hunger Strikers served only to emphasise how tentative any rapprochement was between London and Dublin. Mrs Thatcher was not for turning nor indeed conceding to any of the demands being made by the hunger strikers. Her government continued to determine that treating Irish republicans as criminals was the only way to deal with them.

---

[45]Dwyer, T. Ryle, *Haughey's Thirty Years of Controversy*, Mercier Press, 1993, p. 74

Haughey, by all accounts, was particularly unlucky in this period running up to his first general election. He tried to glean credit from the Summit with Thatcher, but the media were skeptical about any actual change the British might be prepared to entertain. Concessions, if any, were of a minor behind-the-scenes nature. Despite Haughey's efforts at hype, the public were left confused at best by any apparent changes. What had been agreed was something of a long-term change that was to bear fruit many years later with the Anglo-Irish agreement of 1985 and again with the changes in the peace process in the 1990s.

Haughey turned out to be doubly unlucky when tragedy struck in the heart of his own north side with the deaths of 48 teenagers in the Stardust nightclub fire. This happened on the day Haughey's party Ard Fhéis was due to begin in Dublin in mid February 1981. It was to be his launch pad for re-election and with the cancellation of the party conference due to the nightclub deaths there was now no chance of an early general election. Having been denied this chance of an early election he was then exposed to the events in the H-Blocks.

Haughey did make efforts to get Thatcher to compromise on the Hunger Strike issue. According to my father, in a review of Mrs Thatcher's autobiography published in the *Irish Press*: "For five months until Bobby Sands's death in May, the Taoiseach and I tried every device and contact open to us, as did the late Cardinal Ó'Fiaich, the Irish Commission for Justice and Peace, the European Commission on Human Rights, and Michael Foot MP, then leader of the British Labour Party, but to no avail. Lady Thatcher was adamant but her intransigence gave a new lease of life to the Provisional IRA."[46]

Quite apart from his efforts to draw credit from trying to resolve the situation in the north, Haughey found that in the 1981 general election, held in June, his earlier

[46]Brian Lenihan book review of *Thatcher - The Downing Street Years* in the *Irish Press*, October 1993

decision to first embrace and then abandon the cause of fiscal rectitude was to come back and haunt him as an issue as well. Unemployment had increased and inflation was at 21%. In the general election of June 1981 Fianna Fáil under Haughey were to win 45.3% of the votes cast. It was a drop of 5% on the percentage attained by Lynch in 1977. If the 1977 election result is taken as a once off then the Haughey performance, after just over a year and a half in office, is quite good. He suffered a loss of only five seats. Some of these losses could be attributed to the Hunger Strikes and candidates running on Anti H-Block tickets and the rest an inevitability given the soaring and unrealistic victory Lynch had enjoyed in 1977. In contrast, the Fine Gael vote under Garret FitzGerald went up 6% and he gained some 20 seats. Fine Gael and Labour would form a government thus bringing to an end Haughey's first period in power as Taoiseach. Since his arrival in power, Haughey had a confrontational relationship with the media. In the general election campaign TV interviews, Haughey dealt uncomfortably with the, sometimes aggressive, probing from journalists. His media appearances did him no favours.

Haughey's first spell in power had been patchy to say the least of it. In effect, he undermined the goodwill that should have come to him from the Summits with Thatcher by being seen to be over-hyping the results. In doing this, he managed to sow distrust amongst his interlocutors – the British. He also managed to create a few more enemies in the media by being seen to play them in terms of the significance he was trying to orchestrate around the summit events with Thatcher. The media for the most part remained unimpressed by what he had achieved. His failure on the north was only amplified when it became clear that whatever influence he had gained with the British was now at zero, given his own hype, and Mrs Thatcher's sheer intransigence over the Hunger Strikers. All he could do was sit there, powerless, as the hunger strikers continued to die. His private efforts, behind the scenes, were precisely that – private and unseen by the pubic who were therefore in no position to see him in a positive light. Some would see it as a positive thing that he was more restrained during the Hunger Strike and that he did not exploit the obvious, emotional, tinderbox that it represented to carve out votes for himself with the more republican-minded voter. Others suggested that if he had been more robust with the British then it might have given him additional leverage at a later stage.

Haughey was also dogged, in office, by the fact that he led a clearly divided party. The bitterness engendered by the method of his victory in the leadership contest had left a bad taste in the mouths of some of his party members. Equally his inability to be able to adequately sanction George Colley for his pledge of 'qualified loyalty' to Haughey as leader allowed a good number of those on the losing side of the leadership contest to think of Haughey as simply a leader who was there but could be soon removed. A number of Haughey's backbench appointments to junior ministerial positions had also become a source of embarrassment to him in the news media. This added to the impression that he was a bad judge of people when it came to public office. It also allowed some people who opposed him anyhow to depict his victory as one for the 'yahoo' tendency in the party.

Haughey, in this his first term as Taoiseach, also served to disappoint his greatest followers who believed he would bring his business and financial acumen to the position of Taoiseach. Charlie McCreevy, one of the famous gang of five, was soon to become the most vocal of internal critics on this and other matters. The potential gains from Haughey's state of the nation address had been essentially frittered away within months of the brave declaration being made. The public finances were to become the issue in public life for quite a number of years to come. The media were now much less ready to accept bland assurances from government on these matters and were now more than willing to pick holes in the figures presented by any of the political parties that were contending for power.

Haughey also suffered in this period precisely because he had abolished the Department of Public Planning along with its progenitor Martin O'Donoghue. The spare officials were brought into a greatly enlarged Department of the Taoiseach that allowed critics to depict Haughey as taking all power onto himself. The expansion in the Department of the Taoiseach was probably an inevitable trend but the fact that he had been hastened forward so rapidly probably created unease in some quarters. Haughey also had a habit of micromanaging particular departments and interfering in individual departments. This created some degree of turbulence with his own ministers. My father often remarked that his first challenge in any new ministry given to him by Haughey was to identify the Haughey mole in the department. He tended to keep an unusually interested eye in the goings on in particular departments, and in this period on the Department of Foreign Affairs where my father was minister.

Haughey, unduly influenced by Blaney, had taken a kind of hostile view of the department as not being pro-nationalist enough. His attitude was not dissimilar to traditional Tory attitudes to the Foreign Office in the UK. Haughey wanted to move Sean Donlon from his position as the Irish Ambassador in Washington, influenced of course by his sometime mentor Neil Blaney. Donlon had created a consensus with Democrat figures like Ted Kennedy and Tipp O'Neill with regard to how Irish issues would be handled in the States. As Donlon had done a good job cultivating people in Washington, my father was loathe to have him changed. In any event, word began to emerge in the media that Haughey wanted him moved. This proved counter productive both for Haughey and others who wanted Donlon moved. Irish America voiced its dissatisfaction in very blunt terms forcing Haughey to back off. Donlon stayed and in staying demonstrated both the pointlessness of Haughey's efforts to move him but also cast a sidelight on his meddlesome efforts to interfere in line departments, rather than letting his ministers get on with things. My father was hugely annoyed in this period that he was not left to his own devices to manage Iveagh House as he would have wished. Other ministers, who had got used to the Jack Lynch laissez-faire approach, were probably equally annoyed at interference in their departments by Haughey.

Haughey's efforts to micromanage individual departments was very much in evidence in this his first term in office with regard to the economy. His first appointment to the Department of Finance was Michael O'Kennedy who, despite his seniority, was unable to shake off the impression that in fact it was Haughey who was pulling the strings in his department. In any event O'Kennedy was on the way out of government to take up the position of European Commissioner in December of 1980. O'Kennedy was then replaced by Gene FitzGerald of Cork whose previous experience as Minister for Labour did not make him credible in the office. The perception that Haughey himself was running the Department of Finance grew both outside of government circles as well as within. If Haughey thought he had had a rough time of it in Opposition, the next two years were to severely test him with three general elections (including 1981) within a period of 18 months. There were to be a number of direct challenges to his leadership from people within Fianna Fáil whom he had come to loathe and dislike a great deal.

CHAPTER TEN

DISSIDENTS

Garret FitzGerald was now Taoiseach, and by the day, becoming a formidable adversary for Haughey. FitzGerald had a sort of absent-minded professor image, which his PR handlers had managed to turn around. His spin doctors were an extremely talented group of individuals including the late Bill O'Herlihy who subsequently went on to become a TV host of the very popular RTÉ programme that went out every time the Irish soccer team were playing an international. O'Herlihy along with Peter Prendergast (Government Press Secretary), Pat Heneghan (PR) and Enda Marren, a solicitor, went on to become labelled 'the national handlers'. Haughey, now in opposition, tried to depict these men as a sort of cabal who were manipulating Garret and attempting to trick the public into thinking he was much better than he actually was. The fact of the matter was they were highly effective and the media messages they deployed rendered the somewhat bumbling FitzGerald into a sort of nice guy who was hugely intelligent and full of integrity. The integrity card was played with great skill as a sort of contrast to Haughey. These PR handlers created an environment where Garret was depicted as a sort of virtuous Luke Skywalker to Haughey's Darth Vader. In effect, they made Haughey the enemy, the person that everyone wanted to fight against. It was pantomime stuff but it worked to the detriment of Haughey. They also framed the public debate in terms of the country's finances, depicting Haughey as the reckless one, who had played fast and loose with public spending. Garret became the foremost advocate of 'fiscal rectitude'. FitzGerald expressed outrage at the state of the books as soon as he came into office. FitzGerald, in effect, accused Haughey of "cooking the books". According to T. Ryle Dwyer, "the Budget figures presented to the Dáil for 1981 really bore little relationship to the country's economic position".[47] By the time the election happened in June 1981 most of the money allocated had now being spent. FitzGerald brought forward a supplementary estimate, in effect, to raise more money so that the spending profile promised could be met. He loudly complained that Haughey had left the cupboard bare.

If FitzGerald was becoming a significant external critic then Charlie McCreevy, formerly of the Gang of Five who had put Haughey in his position, was now taking up the cudgels against him internally, pleading that his performance in opposition was abysmal. "We seem to be against everything and for nothing," claimed McCreevy. The criticism from McCreevy clearly got on Haughey's nerves. Haughey promptly asked that McCreevy be expelled from the parliamentary party. Many of Haughey's front bench disagreed with him and thought it better to censure McCreevy. Haughey was now being restricted by his own front bench. McCreevy, seeing that he might face disciplinary action, resigned the party whip of his own volition rather than push things to a vote. McCreevy was now a national celebrity and a person that people outside of politics began to hugely admire for his honesty and courage in standing up to Haughey. McCreevy was only out on a limb and outside the parliamentary party for a short while as the FitzGerald government unexpectedly collapsed in February

---

[47]Dwyer, T. Ryle, *Haughey's Thirty Years of Controversy*, Mercier Press, 1992, p. 81

1982 on its own budget, having misjudged the reaction from independents, on whom the government depended for its support. Prior to this, Haughey had repeatedly predicted that the FitzGerald government was unstable and teetering on the brink of collapse. He had annoyed his own party by delaying the appointment of a front bench team, using this pretext. When he did eventually appoint a front bench team half of his parliamentary party got some job or other. It caused more annoyance to his former cabinet colleagues but it showed he was so uncertain in his position as leader he was afraid to offend anyone.

Before the general election of February 1982 could be called, Haughey tried, in vain, to persuade President Patrick Hillery to avoid an election by giving him the opportunity to form a government from within the Dáil. Haughey was right in his judgment but, according to my father, Hillery was not going to accede to this kind of request. Hillery's refusal to take his calls left Haughey in a right temper. In the event, he got my father and Sylvester Barrett (another friend of Hillery) to make contact with the President. Haughey was known for his tantrums with colleagues at this stage. When he detected a reluctance on the part of the front bench colleagues he would take it as a sign of insubordination. He was vulnerable in his position, following the loss of power and was in his temper expressing this frustration. My father and Sylvie [as he was familiarly known] repaired to the members' bar to share a drink after the front bench meeting, neither man realising the storm this incident would generate in years to come. Sylvie and my father cast their eyes to heaven at the notion Haughey was promulgating. They knew Hillery, who was very conservative, would have nothing to do with Haughey's plan, which by its nature was risky as it involved using a power the President had, but for which there was no previous precedent. My father felt Hillery was unlikely to innovate in this manner even if he was to be perfectly within his mandate as President. My father had maintained a strong friendship with Hillery through the Arms Trial and afterwards. It was my father who persuaded Hillery to relinquish his post in Brussels early in order to become an agreed, cross-party nominee, for the position of President following the resignation of Cearbhall Ó'Dálaigh from the job. Nobody wanted an election, least of all the then Fine Gael-Labour Coalition government. But Hillery granted the dissolution of the Dáil and an election was called for February 18th.

The February 1982 general election was an extraordinary event. It was a winter election of dark nights and televised debates. Fianna Fáil went into the election a deeply divided party, with many senior front bench members unhappy with Haughey. Martin O'Donoghue had been invited back on the basis that the party would not seek to exceed the spending levels set by the FitzGerald government. Haughey, in the early days of the election, clearly indicated he was going to breach these figures. O'Donoghue and others were furious at him, forcing him to back down and accept the FitzGerald government ceiling on spending. My father and Ray MacSharry were equally unhappy with Haughey's failure to embrace financial responsibility. Between his tantrums and changes of mind quite a number of his own front benchers were re-appraising his value as leader. Haughey's rating was now badly trailing that of FitzGerald. By the end of the campaign, Irish Marketing Surveys showed 56% of those polled wanted FitzGerald as Taoiseach as opposed to just 33% for Haughey. "Midway through the campaign, his picture was quietly dropped from much of the party's literature."[48] Canvassing the doorsteps for my father in the Dublin West constituency, we were frequently told "we would vote for your father but not for your leader". It was soul-destroying work. Some canvassers would try to claim that this line about our leader was being peddled by Fine Gael, but it was obvious that some of the people saying this were sincere. In fact the great majority of those saying this on the doorsteps had run out of patience

---

[48]Joyce, Joe and Murtagh, Peter, *The Boss*, Poolbeg Press, 1983

with Haughey. We were given canvassing instructions to underplay Haughey and highlight the party as we talked to voters. The Haughey photos, so prominent in 1981, were now vanishing from the personal literature that candidates handed out about themselves. The big posters of him were also distinctly absent. My father found this aspect of the campaign amusing but necessary.

In many constituencies up and down the country, Fianna Fáil candidates were putting themselves forward for election for quite opposite purposes. In Dublin South, Séamus Brennan, an acknowledged opponent of Haughey, was pushing for votes on the basis that if he were elected he would be getting rid of Haughey. Niall Andrews, his running mate, was putting himself forward as a Haughey supporter. It was like this in many different constituencies. Given Haughey's relative unpopularity, as measured by opinion polls, one might have assumed Fianna Fáil were going to take a hiding in the actual election. In fact when the votes were counted the party's share of the vote had gone up by 2% yielding an extra four seats. The intense internal rivalry and division within the party had perversely brought out the party vote. Since the Fianna Fáil seats exceeded that of both Fine Gael and Labour combined, Haughey was now in pole position to form a government from what was a hung Dáil. Haughey would have to negotiate with Independents to form a minority administration. Before doing that he would have to face down a challenge from within his party from none other than Des O'Malley.

In the aftermath of the election the dissident or anti-Haughey faction clearly wanted to mount a challenge to Haughey now that there was a prospect of going into power. Jim Gibbons, Haughey's old nemesis from the Arms Trial, was back in the Dáil and stated on television on election night that there would be a challenge to Haughey's leadership. The dissidents, for their part, wanted to ditch George Colley and rally their forces around Des O'Malley who would have greater appeal, as well as appealing to younger deputies.

Haughey was already sounding out backbench opinion as well as his front bench colleagues. Martin O'Donoghue was having conversations with Albert Reynolds who in turn was seeking to involve Ray MacSharry in the discussions. O'Donoghue was trying to arrange a consensus of senior figures to achieve a change in the leadership. Murtagh and Joyce take up the story in their book *The Boss*:

> *"At about the same time that Tuesday night when O'Donoghue was talking to Reynolds, Haughey was holding his first meeting with Tony Gregory. Before he met Gregory, Haughey instructed Ray Burke and Brian Lenihan to go to O'Malley and find out definitely if a challenge was going to take place. Burke and Lenihan met O'Malley in an unoccupied house in Clonskeagh which he had been able to borrow. The meeting lasted for about an hour but their efforts were fruitless. O'Malley said he was determined to stand against Haughey."*[49]

My father and Ray Burke were aghast at O'Malley's decision. Ray Burke had been a junior minister in O'Malley's department prior to Haughey's victory in the leadership contest in 1979. He and O'Malley had been quite friendly and under O'Malley's influence Burke had voted for Colley. While my father had voted for Haughey he had maintained a friendship with O'Malley. Both families holidayed in Connemara in the summers and we were frequently organising joint barbecues in the company of Bobby Molloy and others. The authors Murtagh and Joyce have captured the gist of the meeting in Clonskeagh but cannot have known the full import of these discussions. Both my father and Ray Burke had decided to put a proposition to O'Malley that was not part of the mandate given to them by Haughey. Both my father and Ray Burke were also a little fed up with Haughey and were in fact ready to contemplate a change of leadership. My father told me that at the meeting in Clonskeagh, he and Burke

[49]Ibid, p. 35

had offered O'Malley their support for the leadership if he would let the challenge go on this occasion so that the party could get into government. The clear import of what they were offering O'Malley was that they could ditch Haughey once a decent interval had occurred between the election and the likelihood of another general election. My father was amazed at O'Malley's lack of political judgment. Here he had two Dublin based ministers of significant influence offering him the leadership if he would just bide his time a little. O'Malley for his part must have been suspicious of the offer, seeing it perhaps as another Haughey ploy. It wasn't, but now my father and Burke had no choice but to back Haughey to the hilt. They both felt a leadership challenge would only jeopardise the party's prospects of negotiating with the independents and winning power. It is clear that others, including MacSharry and Albert Reynolds, were also contemplating a leadership change at this time. Martin O'Donoghue was annoyed with O'Malley for a period of time because of his decision to pursue this possibility. His instincts were not incorrect.

As things turned out, the O'Malley challenge was about to fall on its face, through poor co-ordination, paranoia and plain stupidity on their part. At one point Séamus Brennan believed a Post Office workman's hut placed outside his home was in fact a surveillance crew sent there by Haughey. McCreevy found Haughey aide, P.J. Mara, hanging around near the conspirators' Setanta House offices, in the vicinity of Leinster House, and suspected him of being engaged in keeping an eye on who was going in and out. In the meantime Ray MacSharry and my father came down four square in support of Haughey making it clear that now was not the right time for a leadership challenge. Liam Lawlor, presumed to be an O'Malley supporter, also looked like he was backing Haughey. This seems to have spooked O'Malley a great deal since he had clearly got a pledge of support from Lawlor. Martin O'Donoghue was then accused by the conspirators of pursuing the wrong strategy at the wrong time, when in fact his approach of getting other serious people involved was far more likely to succeed, albeit over a slightly prolonged timeframe. There was now a rift amongst those seeking to get rid of Haughey. O'Donoghue ended up urging O'Malley to withdraw his challenge at the party meeting. The conspirators' plans were now in tatters and O'Malley now got to his feet and withdrew his challenge. O'Donoghue, who had shown far deeper political insight than the others, was nonetheless criticised for his stance, something which deeply upset him. Haughey now had a mandate from the party to negotiate with the independents to form a government.

Haughey took personal control over his discussions with the anti-drug campaigner and Independent deputy for Dublin Central, Tony Gregory. Gregory was a new TD but with a prodigious reputation as a street level, community activist, with roots in the republican movement, where he had been a member of the Irish National Liberation Army (INLA) and its political wing the Irish Republican Socialist Party (IRSP). He was close to this movement's charismatic leader Seamus Costello, the subject of a particularly nasty assassination. Gregory ran a very hard bargain. Haughey kept saying he was "pushing at an open door". The price tag of the Gregory deal for the inner city ran to over a hundred million pounds. In the context of high unemployment and spending cuts it was to cause outrage in the Dáil when Gregory read its details into the Dáil record. It was resented at a wider level that one independent could leverage such resources for his own constituency. Haughey wanted to get into power and was ready to pay any price in order to achieve his aim. My father was not too happy with the Gregory deal either. He could see Haughey's desire to have certainty but was a little annoyed that he had put in place a better deal with the Workers Party, which offered greater stability for the government over a longer period. Haughey's formal consultations with the Workers Party Leader Tomás MacGiolla had gone nowhere. Murtagh and Joyce take up the story; "Behind all the formalities, however, there was another level to the discussions between the Workers' Party and Fianna Fáil. A secret meeting had been arranged by people with contact in both parties and was held in the Gresham Hotel in Dublin between Brian Lenihan and the general secretary of the Workers' Party, Seán Garland."[50]

Seán Garland was and remains something of a legend. He had led a famous raid against an RUC barracks in the North in the 1950s in the company of Seán South, the Limerick man, who was shot in the raid and the subject of the republican ballad 'Seán South of Garryowen'. When the IRA split into its Marxist Official IRA wing and its non-Marxist Provisional Wing Garland had opted to stay with the then IRA Chief of Staff Cathal Goulding. They then went on to form the Workers Party which was bedeviled by allegations that it still maintained an armed wing, the official IRA, under the direction of Garland and others. My father knew Garland and respected him, if not entirely sharing his political agenda. The party leader in the Dáil, MacGiolla, and the Dáil deputies, at this point in the 1980s, in classic Marxist Leninist terms took their instructions directly from the general secretary of the party Seán Garland, and had little or no room to disagree. My father ironed out a deal that would carry the Haughey-led government for a period of three years. Garland put very few preconditions on his offer. The Workers Party had a strong campaigning edge and the onset of two general elections in quick succession had left its activist base tired. Garland adjudged now was as good a time as ever to give themselves a rest. My father trusted Garland and had a prior meeting with him in a house in Leixlip before the meeting in the Gresham. He felt a formal, centrally controlled, party would offer a better chance of stability than relying on independents, whom at that point could be jumpy, troublesome and likely to change their minds under the pressure of public opinion. Haughey's government was to be his most ill-fated to date.

---

[50]Joyce, Joe and Murtagh, Peter, *The Boss*, Poolbeg Press, 1983, p. 54

It was to last just nine months, nine months of unrelenting turbulence.

Haughey, against my father's advice, decided to give the European Commission job to a Fine Gael deputy and former Minister Richard Burke. Burke had been a latecomer to my father's Dublin West constituency. Burke was no fan of Dr Garret FitzGerald and despite an early refusal to take the job eventually accepted Haughey's offer. The benefit of giving Richard Burke the job was that it would put the combined opposition down one seat with the prospect of a two seat gain if Fianna Fáil won the by-election. This, in theory at least, would make the Government more stable. My father knew the figures in his own constituency and did not believe the party could win the seat. His prediction proved to be correct. Jim Mitchell, his Fine Gael opposite number in the constituency, plucked a virtually unknown candidate Liam Skelly from obscurity, but packaged him correctly to make him a winner. Between Jim Mitchell's political nous, knowledge of the ground and the input of the 'national handlers' the Fine Gael machine went into over drive. Haughey ended up more damaged than before. What was conceived as a 'stroke' was now seen to have been a 'stroke' that had not just failed but boomeranged. My father was appointed Minister for Agriculture in this short-lived administration because of the importance Haughey put on getting sensitive farm price discussions to a finality that suited Ireland and the Irish farmers. My father, from his two spells in Foreign Affairs, had huge knowledge about how Europe worked and his own network to rely upon. My father could not have known how lucky he was to have been taken out of the Department of Foreign Affairs at this time. Haughey was to embark on another ill-fated venture, this time, in relation to Mrs Thatcher's war to reverse the invasion of the Falkland Islands by the Argentinian Military Junta.

Mrs Thatcher, with the same determination with which she had defeated the Miners dispute, was of the view that the invasion of the British islands in the desolate South Atlantic should not be allowed to go unpunished. Lord Peter Carrington, her Foreign Secretary, a friend of my father, had resigned because of the Foreign Office's failure to warn of the Argentinian threat. Few in the foreign policy scene, including my father, regarded Haughey's decision to oppose the British over their action to re-capture the islands as a wise move. The policy pursued was justified by Haughey as an expression of our independence in Foreign policy terms. The fact that Haughey's own Defence Minister, Paddy Power, had made bellicose noises on the issue, alongside Neil Blaney, seems to have led to a knee-jerk response by Haughey. There was a sense of euphoria in Britain over the war and Haughey's diplomatic démarche (at the time we had a seat on the UN's Security Council) was taken very badly. My father's concern was that, at a time of serious unemployment, the move by Haughey was bound to damage our trade relationships and set us back in business terms. Britain was then, as she is now, a major trading partner.

The Haughey government was becoming increasingly unpopular. Haughey appeared to be dogged by bad luck as well as bad judgment. In a bizarre twist to things in the summer of 1982 there were a series of random murders that were being attributed, by the Gardaí, to the same single individual. A nurse was killed while sunbathing in a secluded spot in the Phoenix Park and a farmer killed with his own shotgun in the midlands. The two incidents induced paranoia over the summer with a sense of fear and loathing amongst the public. The media had little else to report and the murders were to take even more dramatic turn. The murderer, Malcolm MacArthur, it emerged had been arrested in an apartment owned by Haughey's Attorney General, the legal advisor to the government. This unleashed a spate of false rumours. MacArthur, it seems was a house guest of the Attorney General and had even accompanied him to a GAA match in Croke Park where he had sat alongside leading members of the Gardaí, while a nationwide manhunt for him was underway. It was a huge and unfortunate coincidence with the Attorney General unaware of his houseguest's deeds. Such was the intensity of this summer controversy that the Attorney General resigned rather than bring more undue negative publicity on the government.

At a press conference at the height of the controversy Haughey declared the whole thing "Grotesque, unbelievable, bizarre and unprecedented". His intellectual nemesis of long standing, Dr Conor Cruise O'Brien, was quick to fix his eye on this particular quote and in his columns, proceeded to nickname Haughey and his government as the GUBU Government – grotesque, unbelievable, bizarre and unprecedented. Anytime Haughey got into trouble after this date, Cruise O'Brien would dust off the GUBU acronym and put it to good use in print. So it proved to be. The government was about to fall but not before one Charlie McCreevy decided, off his own bat it appears, to put down a motion of 'No Confidence' in Haughey's leadership.

This motion, unlike its predecessor, was set to be fully debated through the evening and resulted in a victory margin of 58 votes to 22 in Haughey's favour. Haughey had insisted on a full roll-call vote of party TDs. Jack Lynch had done the same in the wake of the Arms Trial. The dissidents depicted this move on his part as anti-democratic despite the previous Lynch precedent that they would have been involved. Des O'Malley, the heir presumptive if the motion had gone against Haughey, was furious about the speed and lack of consultation by McCreevy in putting down his motion. It appears, in relation to this challenge again, that there was very poor co-ordination amongst the likely beneficiaries from a leadership change. McCreevy was depicted as a maverick on a solo run.

"Haughey had his argument worked out. In summary, he declared that there was terrible disloyalty to the party leader, people were working against him, and the grass roots were furious with those involved. He claimed that the party membership was entitled to know who was voting against him as leader," according to Des O'Malley in his autobiography.[51] Haughey, recognising the threat, took the gloves off and instead of purely relying on the support of party big wigs like my father and Ray MacSharry made a direct appeal to the party organisation. In the previous, failed, O'Malley heave he had done a little of this. On this occasion he mobilised all of his formidable, constituency party resources as well as those available to him at a national level. The dissidents complained of undue pressure and actual intimidation. Certainly Haughey supporters were lining up and putting individual TDs under pressure to support him. "As for the pressure used by his supporters, it was beyond anything previously known in Irish politics: sinister late-night phone calls; financial manipulation, threatening livelihoods on the one hand and discharging debts on the other,"[52] according to Des O'Malley. In my, rather more humble, experience as an ordinary member of the party at this time, real feelings ran high. The dissident versus Haughey conflict had percolated to almost every branch of the organisation. The ordinary members, up to this point, were passive spectators in what was a game of rival elites within the party. Haughey's invitation was avidly taken up at the grass roots level because it was perhaps one of the few occasions since the Arms Trial they were actually invited to venture their own opinion. It was an unrivalled opportunity for ordinary activists to tell their so-called elders and betters what to do.

The outpouring of anger, support and complaint from the rank and file was inevitable given the indiscipline they had seen from the senior members of the party and the parliamentary party generally. They were also, in a curious way, mimicking the tactics and antics of the parliamentary

[51]O'Malley, Desmond *Conduct Unbecoming – A Memoir*, Gill & Macmillan, 2014, p..136
[52]O'Malley, Desmond *Conduct Unbecoming – A Memoir*, Gill & Macmillan, 2014, p..136

party itself. In the Kevin Barry Cumann, of which I was a member when at UCD, most of the membership was split along the same lines as the parliamentary party. One officer board member had written to a national newspaper indicating his opposition to Haughey. This caused a ritual and virulent denunciation of him by the membership and officer board who felt he was not entitled to do this as it had not been discussed by the Cumann in its own right. There was also annoyance amongst activists at the way in which the dissidents worked so closely with the media and seemed to be prepared to form an alliance with them against our own party leadership. Haughey had this kind of 'direct action' type supporter within the rank and file. Most of them had no relationship with Haughey but were in support of him because of what he stood for – republicanism, capitalism, success. Haughey, typical of his populism, had supporters both on the right and the left of the party. The O'Malley grouping tended to be more sedentary in their habits, armchair activists, and more likely to be overly influenced by what the media might write or say about the party. In a phrase, they seemed to incline more towards the golf club than the GAA. The faction now gathered around O'Malley had previously, under Colley, been consistently incompetent in the way they went about fighting Haughey. They seemed to rely too much on media approval rather than chasing down the votes they needed to achieve their aims. In addition to this, Haughey had a significant record behind him. They, for their part, failed to articulate an alternative narrative to that offered by Haughey. They were in effect seeking power without explaining for what purpose. Unlike FitzGerald who did try to present an alternative narrative to Haughey the dissidents had no particular vision of their own. They were still open to the charge that they had not got over the departure of Jack Lynch, who himself travelled light when it came to a substantial philosophy.

The November election of 1982 was to be a disaster for the party. On a percentage basis the party's support level was around 45% but they had lost six seats. The really significant shift was that Fine Gael, under Garret FitzGerald, had come perilously close to toppling Fianna Fáil's traditional dominance in Irish electoral politics. Fine Gael's vote of 39% gave them just five seats fewer than Fianna Fáil in the Dáil. Garret FitzGerald would be back as Taoiseach. FitzGerald had very cleverly staked out different ground, emphasising the differences between himself and Haughey. On the north FitzGerald was a conciliator and on the economy against reckless spending. Haughey, through his Falklands escapade, had become a loser on both of these issues. FitzGerald had also pointed to the internal opposition to Haughey as further proof of why Haughey was unfit to hold the office of Taoiseach. Haughey's PR operation was a disaster when compared to the slickness and relentless quality of that which FitzGerald had put in place. FitzGerald had also mobilised a younger, more liberal, voter who was pleased with his vague commitment to a more pluralist Ireland, hinting at progressive change on issues like contraception, divorce and abortion. On the latter issue Garret had panicked, along with Haughey, and promised the pro-life movement a referendum on the issue. FitzGerald was about to be given a sustained period in office to prove his credentials. The battle between Haughey and FitzGerald, which had come to dominate politics, was now set to continue until 1987. Haughey was shortly to experience yet another challenge to his leadership, this time while he was in opposition.

CHAPTER ELEVEN

OPPOSITION

In December of 1982 Garret FitzGerald had a new Minister for Justice. His name was Michael Noonan, and he was from Limerick. Soon after taking office he had asked his officials if the phones of two prominent journalists, Bruce Arnold and Geraldine Kennedy, had been the subjects of Garda wiretaps. They quickly confirmed that these phones had been tapped. Rumours had been sweeping around about the matter and the *Irish Times* had printed a story on the issue following the November 1982 election. Noonan promptly gathered his evidence, interviewed the Garda Commissioner Patrick McLaughlin and his Assistant Commissioner in charge of Security and Intelligence Branch Joe Ainsworth.

As a result of Noonan's investigation, McLaughlin and Ainsworth left office. At the time Noonan claimed that neither man was encouraged to resign or retire, but State papers released in 2013 under the 30 year rule revealed that McLaughlin drafted a letter to Noonan indicating that he felt he must retire as "it is apparent that you and the Government feel that I have not lived up adequately to my responsibilities". The same release of papers from the National Archives contained draft minutes from the Department of An Taoiseach entitled 'Removal of Commissioner and Deputy Commissioner from Office' indicating Noonan's apparent wish that they step down.

Meanwhile, former Minister for Justice Seán Doherty was also in deep trouble. Doherty had initiated the wiretaps during Charles Haughey's ill-fated nine month term in office the previous year. Haughey issued an immediate denial that he had in any way sanctioned the wiretaps. But the tapping of the journalists' phones and a separate tape-recording by Haughey's then Tánaiste, Ray MacSharry, of a conversation he had with his ministerial colleague, Martin O'Donoghue, were to be the subject of lasting controversy and heated debate. The controversy over the taped conversation with O'Donoghue was centred on the fact that O'Donoghue seemed to be suggesting in the recording that if any of those who were loyal to Haughey were financially compromised, then he knew of people who were prepared to fund TDs who were in that difficulty. TDs were uneasy with the notion that money was somehow available, with Haughey and his supporters pushing the line that in effect money was being made available to compromise people in their voting decisions. This was ironic given that the same allegation had been made against Haughey in the internal Fianna Fáil leadership battle of 1979. Meanwhile, the dissidents within the party focused on the tapping of the two journalists' phones and saw this as the last straw. Phone tapping was normally reserved as a measure to investigate serious crime or threats to the security of the state but on this occasion the gardaí were under orders from a minister which they felt they could not ignore. Party dissidents launched yet another attempt to get rid of Haughey. This was by far their best chance to date.

Haughey's situation was seen to be so bad that the *Irish Press,* a paper set up by Fianna Fáil, published his political obituary rather than be beaten to the story by other newspapers. The publication by the *Irish Press* poisoned the subsequent relationship between the paper and the party. Haughey, it was said, was on the brink of resignation. One suggestion is made that he was about to do so but was dissuaded from doing so by his old friend Neil Blaney. Blaney has admitted as much: "He, effectively, had resigned. The resignation was written out."[53] My father has said of the time that Haughey had completely caved in and Blaney had been contacted by close friends of Haughey to put some fight back into him. Haughey gathered together some of his key people, including my father, into a small group to prepare their tactics and to defend themselves against this latest attack. Michael O'Kennedy, operating on the assumption that Haughey was in fact going to resign the leadership, let it be known that he would be a candidate to succeed him. Seizing on this, my father and P.J. Mara advised that they needed to get more candidates into the field in order to confuse things, the idea being to make TDs uneasy by demonstrating that choosing a replacement to Haughey might not be all that simple. O'Kennedy would make it a two-way contest involving himself and O'Malley. However if more candidates could be got into the field then the ordinary TDs would see a more difficult succession process, one that was likely to be more divisive than imagined. The implication was clear – Des O'Malley was not going to get a clear run at the leadership.

An early meeting of the parliamentary party had concluded with TDs presuming Haughey was gone but that he should be allowed to go with a bit of dignity. This, as Des O'Malley has acknowledged, was a mistake on the part of those seeking to get rid of him. Haughey and his team needed to string out consideration of his leadership. An internal party inquiry into the whole telephone-tapping affair had begun and Haughey's aides were insisting that this had to report before the leadership matter could be looked into. Apart

[53]Rafter, Kevin, *Neil Blaney – A Soldier of Destiny*, Blackwater Press, 1993

from O'Malley and O'Kennedy, there were no others so far declaring an interest in replacing Haughey. Gerry Collins, his former Foreign Minister, and original campaigner for Colley, was in hospital. Raymond Smith takes up the story of Haughey's visit to him:

> *"Haughey, not alone confided in Gerry Collins that he intended resigning but he spent forty-five minutes urging the Limerick West Deputy to allow his name to go forward as a contender for the leadership. He even went so far as to express the view that he thought that Gerry Collins would make an excellent leader and was, in fact, the only person he saw in the Parliamentary Party as capable of leading the Party out of its difficulties at that time."*[54]

The pitch by Haughey was a clever one and part of a wider effort to send the message to potential O'Malley supporters that their man was not certain to win. Collins was initially cautious about Haughey's prompting but eventually relented. The next day he arranged to be photographed from his hospital bed, looking hale and hearty in a national newspaper, which suggested he would be a candidate for the vacancy Haughey was going to create. This was greeted with a degree of incredulity by those in the Haughey camp but served to undermine O'Malley using someone who had previously been a key ally.

The leadership race was now becoming a crowded field. My father and the rest of the campaign team then proceeded to throw in the names of other potential leadership candidates and John Wilson, a border county minister, an avuncular senior figure, was encouraged to throw his hat in the ring. The fact that there were now two other candidates from the Munster region did much to damage O'Malley's capability to carry Munster in a leadership contest. In all of this, Haughey was suddenly given a breather from the inevitable

[54]Smith, Raymond, *Haughey & O'Malley – The Quest for Power*, Aherlow Publishers, 1986, p. 159

defeat that everyone was predicting. Clem Coughlan, a TD from Donegal, was tragically killed in a car crash. The party meeting was adjourned for the following week after his funeral. Haughey's team went into overdrive. Haughey was on the phone, night and day, to my father. My father asked me to drive him up to Donegal for the Coughlan funeral. After the funeral in a place called Frosses, the TDs who had travelled up repaired to a local hotel in Donegal town, where a meal had been prepared for those mourners who had travelled up for the funeral. The scene in the hotel was frenetic. My father was in a different corner, every minute, with TDs and others button holing him about the situation. There was this small, inner lobby, or space between the dining room and the main lobby at the front of the hotel. After the meal, Haughey positioned himself at the dining room door with his back to the wall. He stood there, motionless, staring straight ahead at nothing in particular. He was on his own.

It was a study in how he deployed himself in a situation of great pressure. He stood there, acknowledging nobody, until they in fact made the first move towards him. I was sitting on a nearby couch observing it all. The famous wavering or 'middle ground' deputies would walk either to or from the dining room. They would suddenly, either become aware of his presence, or catch his eye. Few of his deputies were prepared to pass him, most stopped, looked shifty or embarrassed, but engaged in a word with him here or there. If they were wavering or had said something negative about him they were kind of relieved that he was not taking it too personally and was still talking to them. He said very little, never pitched for support, but offered them a sort of psychological support or a gentle or encouraging tap to the arm or shoulder. If they held his grasp for long he would become lively and animated, feeling he had a chance with this particular deputy. His demeanour was sombre and respectful. In the hour that he stood there he spoke to at least twenty TDs, with only outright opponents having the confidence to ignore him, pass by him, without an acknowledgement of some kind. My father had spoken to him only once and it was an animated discussion about the statement they were to issue from Haughey that night. Haughey was edgy about the content, suspecting it would land him in more trouble.

On the way back in the car my father told me to switch on the car radio to catch the evening time news. My father had crafted the wording, along with others, of this statement that drove the Haughey dissidents wild with paranoia. The statement was a direct appeal to the party organisation. The statement seemed to hint that if Haughey lost the vote in the parliamentary party he would seek to defend his leadership at the party's annual conference or Ard Fhéis. In purely technical terms the leader selected by the parliamentary party must be endorsed by the Ard Fhéis. It has never been the case that the Ard Fhéis has selected anyone else. The appalling vista that this would represent would make deputies uneasy. Then, to make himself all the more dignified, he did a radio interview the following Sunday stating that of course he would accept the verdict of his peers in the parliamentary party. It was a classic part of Haughey's stock and trade to send rumours about himself out so that opponents would take them up. Once they repeated it publicly he would knock down the allegation with supporting facts, making the person issuing the allegation seem malicious in intent. Haughey's interview ahead of the actual debate was a bravura performance. When the veteran broadcaster Gerald Barry stated that his critics said he, Haughey, was the problem in the party he responded: "Well I think my critics are the problem in the Party, and I think we could all identify, many people now clearly identify, where the basic problem in the party is. I was elected as leader of the Party by a democratic majority, a small majority, and the people who were beaten at that time have never accepted the situation and have constituted themselves as a group within the Party ever since, anxious to avail of any opportunity to exploit any position that arises to damage me as leader of the party."

Haughey had acquired, over the years, some very clever advisors and he was always prepared to listen to their ideas and see which approach or opinion suited him best. At a political level, at this time, Ray MacSharry and my father were instrumental in saving him from defeat. There were others apart from these two. People like Albert Reynolds and Pádraig Flynn, to mention just two, had spent years orchestrating campaigns and along with others knew pretty much every trick in the book. The famous Gang of Five who had taken out Jack Lynch were a sophisticated and shrewd bunch. They were particularly expert at moving around and pretending they were on one side or the other to gain better insight. One particular trick they regularly employed over these various challenges was the classic of allowing one of their own to go rogue early on in a contest so that they could soak up as much information as possible from the rival campaign. The 'plant' in the rival campaign would go missing at vital moments, engendering paranoia and sowing doubts about others. The dissidents were suckers in this regard, often not spotting these types, and embracing them as people who had some genuine conversion to their cause. The transcript from the O'Donoghue conversation with MacSharry was fairly innocuous, but the suggestion that people could be salvaged from their financial distress was ruthlessly exploited by Haughey. He was now accusing the dissidents of trying to buy off supporters and corruption, something they had been accusing him of for years. The coup de grâce for the dissidents was that on this occasion Haughey permitted a secret ballot. My father thought this one a great wheeze. It allowed people who may have foolishly declared against Haughey in the early part of the crisis to quietly slip back into a position of support with anonymity guaranteed. As Séamus Brennan memorably retorted, when asked why yet again he and the dissidents seemed to have got their numbers wrong: "You can't count moving sheep". Haughey won by 40 to 33.

Haughey had now finally crushed all semblance of internal opposition. People like Séamus Brennan, Charlie McCreevy and Joe Walsh, who had been active dissidents, now recognised that further resistance to Haughey was pointless. They were to stay with Fianna Fáil rather than follow Des O'Malley further and out of the party altogether. Haughey resumed where he had left off in 1981 when finding himself in opposition, that is, defining his role as Opposition leader as opposing for the sake of opposing the government. In this respect he was both amoral and utterly opportunistic.

The pro-life movement had become very vocal in 1982 and pressured both Haughey and FitzGerald into supporting the principle of a constitutional referendum to include a ban on abortion in the constitution. Haughey gave the commitment and FitzGerald, despite his secular crusade, had followed suit. FitzGerald had accepted the Fianna Fáil wording prior to the election but was now entertaining doubts. Peter Sutherland, the then Attorney General, was suggesting the wording might have the opposite effect to that which was intended. Haughey played on the fears of the Pro-Life movement and they in turn ratcheted up the pressure on the government. A number of Fine Gael and Labour TDs voted to re-instate the Fianna Fáil wording. The September 1983 referendum saw Haughey's wording inserted directly into the constitution. This was an early torpedo into the FitzGerald hull, which did much to discredit him with his eager, younger and liberal-minded supporters. Like the dissidents, he had been out-manoeuvred by Haughey. Many of the Pro-Life people became members of Fianna Fáil and an integral part of the Haughey defence team. Haughey became the politician they trusted most on their issue. Though Haughey's lifestyle was, in many ways, at odds with the Catholic ideal.

In 1983 Haughey made an emergency visit to Libya for a meeting with the Libyan leader Muammar Gaddafi. My father had been out there previously and met with the Libyan leader in his traditional Arab tent in the desert. That visit by my father, when Minister for Agriculture, had established the foundation for the Haughey visit. Irish business people in the meat trade, including Seamus Purcell and Larry Goodman, had an interest in re-opening the live cattle trade to that country. The Fine Gael-Labour coalition had been unable to prise open this market. Haughey won a commitment to do so from Gaddafi. It underpinned his credentials enormously that he could simply fly somewhere and do a business deal for Ireland that the government itself could not manage. There were some hilarious stories from the visit. While Haughey waited for Gaddafi, his eye was drawn to the presence of the Libyan leader's team of female bodyguards. These women wore tight, lycra outfits with large pistols strapped to their thighs. There was apparently a sparkle in Haughey's eye as he took in the scene. The bodyguards were strewn around the room, lying languidly on expensive-looking sofas in some cases. It reminded my father of a scene from the James Bond movie *Goldfinger*. Haughey, my father would joke afterwards, must have found the presence of these females and the guns irresistible.

Meanwhile, FitzGerald, in a bid to prop up his efforts on Anglo-Irish relations, created a structure called the New Ireland Forum. It was also designed to prop up the SDLP who were facing a significant challenge from Sinn Féin who were gaining support in the wake of the ten deaths in the 1981 Hunger Strike. It was also an effort to get an agreed approach between the nationalist parties north and south.

Haughey selected a dependable group to be his delegation, including of course, my father and Ray MacSharry. There was a lot of talk about inclusivity and an effort from Garret FitzGerald to suggest that there could be a number of equally valid outcomes in terms of an agreed settlement of the Northern Ireland problem. Haughey made much of the fact that he was under pressure from his own hawks in the delegation with Ray MacSharry being cited as one of these by the media. A lot of it was game playing. The Forum went on for quite a long time. FitzGerald thought he could corner Haughey into his agreed document. My father, for his part, could not believe the naïveté of FitzGerald. When the Forum published its final report, Haughey endorsed it, stating with a degree of hyperbole that all parties had agreed that Irish unity was the most preferred option. It was a misrepresentation of the report's conclusions but Haughey would not be deterred. My father found the whole Forum a rather bizarre thing for an incumbent government to do. Fianna Fáil were only out of power for a year but now the government was giving them a high status, prestige profile, in these solemn plenary sessions up in Dublin Castle. It gave the party an equivalence with the government in terms of national policy. He and the others could not believe their luck. They could also see that the Forum was taking up huge amounts of government time which otherwise should have been focused on getting the economy into good shape. Seamus Mallon would often stay overnight in our home during these sessions. Amongst the SDLP delegation Mallon inclined more to the Fianna Fáil side of things than to Fine Gael. They trusted Haughey more because of his northern family background. Through the Forum my father and Haughey became very friendly with Seán MacBride, the veteran republican, Nobel Prize Winner and former Minister for Foreign Affairs. MacBride became a huge enthusiast for Haughey and privately was the source of marvellous advice.

Fianna Fáil had decided to run a very tight ship with regard to the Forum. Members of the party who were not on the delegation were urged not to express opinions about the north. Des O'Malley, who was not on the delegation, started to make contrary noises about the party's position. This public dissent by O'Malley was not welcomed by parliamentary party members. At the instigation of Haughey, the party whip was removed from O'Malley, who remained a member of the party, but was removed from the parliamentary party. This underlined to everybody that Haughey meant business and was no longer entertaining dissent from any quarter. It was already dawning on O'Malley that his career in Fianna Fáil was all washed up. He chose the occasion of a government bill on contraception, which Haughey was opposing, to stake out his ground and making a speech, which contained the memorable phrase "I stand by the Republic". It positioned O'Malley as a progressive, liberal-minded guy, at odds with the prevailing orthodoxy in Fianna Fáil. Strangely he neither voted for the measure or against it, merely making the speech, and then leaving Leinster House to go to a race meeting. However the protest itself and the failure to vote along with Fianna Fáil was enough for Haughey. He proceeded to insist that O'Malley be expelled from the party organisation, a much more serious step. O'Malley had clung on, outside the parliamentary party, but still a member of the party. O'Malley was now being subjected to treatment that Blaney, Boland and others had received at the time of the Arms Trial – full expulsion from the party altogether. People who tried to reason with Haughey were told bluntly: "It is him or me".

The instruction to the party's national executive was very clear – Haughey wanted him out. Haughey was now utterly tired of being forgiving to his obvious enemies. My father was both apprehensive and a little energised before the meeting of the national executive. My father was a joint Honorary Secretary of the Party and knew a lot about that body's mood. Everyone suspected that O'Malley was probably trying to find a policy issue that would allow him to leave the party with a favourable issue at his back. People were keen to maintain party discipline and make no more excuses for those who wanted to snipe at the party leadership, as the occasion suited them. Over the previous years Haughey had also become conscious of the fact that his own biggest supporters were prone to be disillusioned with him when he did not act the big tough guy upon which his image, to a large extent, now depended. Because of all the party heaves against him he was now seen as a ruthless and rugged survivor. This meant he could no longer afford to be soft and conciliatory towards his internal critics. FitzGerald had a formidable propaganda machine and Haughey had just introduced P.J. Mara to run his publicity machine. Mara was to prove a revelation in the role and for the first time since becoming leader Haughey had someone who could actually get on with the media, feeding them the lines and background stories that they were dying to hear. Mara did a great deal to repair the damage done to Haughey, in media relationship terms, by the dissidents.

As Des O'Malley puts in his book, "Haughey was not interested in technicalities, and the speech was used as an excuse to get me out of the party. In truth, I had come to accept that there was no future for me in Fianna Fáil while Haughey remained as leader"[55]. The party's National Executive voted to expel O'Malley from the party by a margin of 73 votes to 9. Haughey had appealed to them to make it a unanimous decision. Des O'Malley was allowed to address them beforehand. My father as Deputy Leader had been present. Despite the friendship with O'Malley over the years he felt also that this expulsion was necessary if the party was to recover ground against the incumbent FitzGerald government. Afterwards he did

[55]O'Malley, Desmond, *Conduct Unbecoming,* Gill & Macmillan, 2004, p. 152

not endear himself to O'Malley and his waiting supporters by describing it as a 'great night for democracy'. The die was cast in relation to O'Malley. In a matter of months my father and party headquarters moved against the O'Malley political machine in his constituency. The aptly named 'Operation Limerick' involved a high profile visit by my father and others to the city. They arrived by train with members of the local organisation invited to greet them. Though O'Malley was out of the party a lot of the membership were still, understandably, loyal to and part of O'Malley's political machine. My father was there to get them to swear up loyalty to the party leader or face the prospect of also leaving Fianna Fáil. A similar effort to re-organise Dublin South Central was also attempted due to the fact that the local deputy Ben Briscoe had been the sponsor of the motion of no confidence vote on Haughey's leadership. The impression being created was that those who did not salute the party flag were to be the subject of disciplinary measures.

In 1985 Garret FitzGerald wrested, from a very reluctant Mrs Thatcher, a negotiated agreement called the Anglo-Irish Agreement. It was an undoubted diplomatic triumph. It was all the more impressive given that Mrs Thatcher, less than a year prior to this, had in humiliating fashion for FitzGerald ruled out all three of his suggested solutions to the northern problem contained in his New Ireland Forum report. Many had concluded, Haughey presumably also, that the lady was not for turning and probably relished the fact that her "Out, Out, Out" statement had proved an embarrassment for Garret. The new agreement formalised a consultative role for Dublin in the affairs of Northern Ireland that was clearly the intention behind the British concession to the Irish at the Haughey-Thatcher Summit in Dublin Castle. Haughey, in a fit of pique, denounced the agreement without considering the full implications of this position. My father felt his opposition to the agreement was far too negative and knee-jerk. Haughey was still obsessive in his opposition for opposition's sake and hugely motivated about giving FitzGerald no legitimacy on the republican issue.

FitzGerald proved to be a master of communications and propaganda, wrong-footing Charlie, and announcing the deal with a fanfare of international publicity. In a desperate bid to explain his position he asked my father to go out to America and explain the party's opposition to the agreement. My father was one of Ted Kennedy's best friends in Ireland. The Irish-American politicos had been well briefed on the deal by John Hume. There was no point to the mission proposed by Haughey. My father spent the week in America drinking with Kennedy and catching up with his Irish-American contacts. My father quietly told his friends there was no point to the party position and that in all probability, if returned to office, the party would operate the agreement as a given. The only significant information my father appears to have gathered over there was a behind the scenes view on the JFK assassination with a number of insiders he met attributing the Dallas killing to none other than Lyndon B. Johnson, Kennedy's Vice President. The FitzGerald government basked in the reflected glory of this publicity and the diplomatic triumph of the agreement. It gave them a boost in the opinion polls. In some respects it may have even lulled them into a false sense of security. They then proceeded to stage a referendum on the divorce issue. Like most governments they, including FitzGerald, were beginning to succumb to the publicity they themselves generated. In any event FitzGerald was soon to get a rude awakening to reality. The defeat of the Divorce Referendum destroyed the last shard of credibility that FitzGerald enjoyed with regard to his liberal credentials.

"After passage of the Anglo-Irish agreement, the FitzGerald government tried to remove the

constitutional prohibition on divorce in a referendum (25 June 1986). Although Fianna Fáil remained nominally neutral, most party deputies and activists assisted anti-divorce campaigners in defeating the measure. Haughey issued a personal statement expressing his belief in the importance of the family. Years later it was revealed that he had just returned from holidaying with Terry Keane.[56]

Terry Keane was of course Charlie Haughey's long-term mistress. It came as a surprise to me that the relationship had gone back as far as 1972 and was still going right through the 1980s. It was one of the worst-kept secrets of Irish political life. In this period I was a member, subsequently Chairman, of the Kevin Barry Cumann in UCD. The Cumann members were anxious to get Haughey to visit the main Belfield Campus during Freshers' Week, the time when students are enrolled into the student clubs and societies. Repeated requests for him to attend the Cumann for this event had fallen on deaf ears both at party HQ and in Haughey's own office. A few of the officers of the Cumann decided to press our case more fulsomely. We asked to meet his personal secretary and private office staff on the matter. Our letter stated that the campus had become overwhelmingly Fine Gael and that Garret FitzGerald was a frequent and popular visitor to the College. When we got to the office in Leinster House we were told bluntly that for security and other reasons Mr Haughey did not visit college campuses. Apparently he was a significant target for student protesters of all kinds and therefore did not like doing these types of events. Eventually they relented and agreed to a 'controlled' walk about and social reception. His staff rejected the option of a public speech or even a talk at the reception.

---

[56]Maume, Patrick, *Royal Irish Academy Monograph* Dictionary of Irish Biography.

When the day came Haughey appeared. Gardaí and UCD's own security people were on hand to escort him on his visit. We toured him around the usual student stands. It was a marvel to see the reaction of students. He had this personal magnetism that made people excited. The word went out that he was on campus. Within minutes there were throngs of gawking onlookers. People you would hardly expect it from, would be stuck for words, awe struck and become terribly deferential. Haughey had this sense of decorum and deportment that made him the centre of attraction. He did not speak much but when he spoke his comments were timely. Of course Republican and far left protesters were hanging around on the wings, giving an added bit of menace to the walk-about. I had arranged some friends from the UCD Rugby Club to form an inner and outer ring of defence while he moved around. True to form there had been one or two attempts by lone protesters to break through and get to Mr Haughey. Kieran Rigney, a tall number 8 on the UCD team neatly disposed of one such potential assailant. At the reception we had invited not just party members but people from various parts of the college who were well-wishers or worked with us on a day-to-day basis, even if not of the same party political persuasion. Included in the guest list was Madeleine Keane who was in the same year as myself at UCD. Few in the audience knew who she was, even fewer I suspect, that her mother was Haughey's long-term mistress. Haughey seemed totally at ease and relaxed talking to Madeleine. That was the strange thing about Haughey, both in relation to the source of his money and to his mistress; a lot of people knew but were not interested in talking about it. The people who did not know about it simply did not know. A lot of people who did not know about these things put the whole thing down to wild rumour. Ireland is still a place where the wildest and most untruthful rumours can take off in a compelling manner and in an instant. Haughey, to a large extent, benefitted from this prevailing skepticism that Irish people have of stories that are told on the grapevine or social dinner table. Many of the rumours put out about Haughey actually added to his allure in some quarters. There were so many of them going back to the 1960s it was actually hard to keep up with them. The story of his fractured skull, prior to the budget, and the Arms Trial continued to be the subjects of wild speculation even though the Haughey family, since his death, have strenuously denied any improprieties on Haughey's part.

It was only towards the latter end of his long-term affair with Terry Keane that the subject became the source of widespread gossip, wagging tongues and speculative but coded media coverage. Part of the reason for this was a simple one. Terry Keane, herself, invited further intrusion by writing a hugely popular, highly suggestive, social diary with the *Sunday Independent*. It was liberally sprinkled with insider gossip and on many occasions hinted at the writer's access to the man who had again become Taoiseach. The column was called the Keane Edge and it often brought the reader and presumably even Haughey right to the edge in terms of potential disclosure. Anyway, both as a journalist and friend of her daughter, I was frequently in her company. Terry was a very charming person and I believe genuinely in love with Haughey. The affair could not have gone on that long unless there was real respect on both sides. The manner in which she eventually went public about her affair with Haughey was a surprise to many. My own view is that she felt forced to do so because a journalist colleague, Kevin O'Connor, who also worked at the *Sunday Independent*, was promising to publish a book on the affair anyway. This prospect clearly got to her in some respects and she felt it might be better to get the story out ahead of such an eventuality so that her version rather than that of others was heard and accepted. She did not seek to cash in further by turning her serialised articles on the affair into a published book, as appeared to be suggested at the time. Nor did she appear to be a woman scorned by Haughey though he did apparently bring an end to the affair.

Haughey may have been small in stature but he had a huge appetite for taking big risks – in both the sexual and financial arenas. Inevitably people did and have continuously accused him of huge double standards. Haughey himself was blissfully unaware of his own shortcomings and contradictions. In this respect it was easy for people to attribute to him the characteristics of a megalomaniac. He had an enormous sense of himself, a personal egotism, and a belief in his own indestructibility. Unlike his opponent Garret FitzGerald he had not come from a comfortable middle class home with a father who was a minister in the government. His early life saw his father an invalid with Multiple Sclerosis and his mother left to fend for a family of seven children on a modest army pension. Much of his subsequent life, by his own family's admission, was driven by a sense of insecurity that had been brought about by this upbringing. It probably made him tougher and more personally anxious to succeed. In his political life and persona he seems to have perfected a sense of his own ultimate destiny. It may seem slightly delusionary to some but it was clearly strongly felt.

If 1985 was a bad year for Haughey in terms of his rival Garret FitzGerald's success, then the latter half of the year was to bring dramatic evidence of his own indestructibility. To celebrate his 60th birthday Haughey and a few friends chose to sail his yacht, The Taurima, from Dingle to Howth Harbour. Late in the night their yacht collided with a dangerous reef that protrudes unseen out from Mizen Head, the well-known lighthouse and navigational point for sailors. Haughey and his friends were forced to abandon the sinking yacht, to take refuge in the water beneath Mizen's towering rock face. A May Day message had been

sent out from the yacht's radio and after two and half hours
Haughey and the crew were taken away by a rescue boat.
It was during that summer that the whole country was
gripped by a phenomenon described as 'Moving Statues'.
The media and ordinary people could talk of nothing else.
In various parts of Ireland people started reporting that
religious statues were moving and becoming the target of
mass devotions and prayers. The most famous one being
a moving statue in a village called Ballinspittle in County
Cork. It sparked a country-wide spate of similar sightings
of statues that would move. My brother Brian reckoned it
was the church getting their flock ready for an epic contest
over the impending referendum on divorce. Because of this
recrudescence of raw superstition the brother and I reckoned
there was now every chance that Charlie Haughey would be
forgiven and come back to power as Taoiseach. Brian joked
that if people were prepared to believe in moving statues
then there was every chance they might also believe that
Haughey could yet perform economic miracles.

In October 1985 the small airport at Knock in County
Mayo opened to the public. Haughey was invited to do the
opening for this privately-funded initiative by a charismatic,
local, priest called Monsignor Horan. The Dublin-based
commentators had rubbished the whole project as utter
folly and Haughey's support for the project was instanced as
yet another example of his profligacy. Haughey chartered
a small plane to attend the event. My father, the poet Paul
Durcan, coincidentally a nephew of Seán MacBride, and
the *Magill* journalist Gene Kerrigan travelled down for the
event. The opening was a celebration of the determination
that exists in the West, in particular Mayo, the place where
Michael Davitt's land war had begun in the 19th century.
There were mobs of people encircling the airport. There
was both a religious and political fervor to the occasion. At
one point, Paul Durcan, Haughey's invited poet, stood up
to read one of his poems, close in format to a traditional

Catholic prayer. The listening audience, mistaking it for an actual prayer, devotedly uttered the ritual response. My father said it was a great event. In many ways the whole event and issue around Knock Airport sums up Haughey's inveterate populism. He had faced down his critics, largely the Dublin establishment, and backed a project which was now on its way to becoming a demonstrable success. He, the self-styled outsider, was prepared to risk isolation in order to support those who were of the same psychological make-up to himself.

Haughey was proving to be resilient. The election of 1987 was to prove a bitter disappointment for him. In true populist style he denounced the FitzGerald government. The party's slogan in the election was "Health Cuts hurt the old, the sick and the handicapped". It was a play for the protest vote. The irony of course was that Haughey was soon to prove himself most adept, after the election, in imposing draconian cuts and a radical reshaping of government spending. Haughey genuinely felt that on this occasion he would win the elusive majority, which his internal critics used as a stick to beat him with. There were grounds for optimism on his part. FitzGerald had failed on two distinct fronts; his secular crusade for a more pluralist Ireland lay in tatters following the two referenda on Divorce and Abortion; FitzGerald's hope of restoring 'fiscal rectitude' to the public finances was dashed on the rocks of his coalition partner's resistance to the concept. At a key point in FitzGerald's administration Alan Dukes, his Finance minister, tabled a series of adjustments to public spending which when the Labour Party learnt of them they refused to accept. The failure was compounded by the fact that the Labour ministers refused to even discuss them and simply left the cabinet room in protest. That was something of a death knell for FitzGerald's government.

On this occasion Haughey had been robbed of a possible majority thanks to the intervention of his oldest, surviving enemy, namely Des O'Malley. O'Malley's new party the Progressive Democrats had surfed popular anger about high taxation to take 14 seats in the general election. While not all of these seats were at the expense of Fianna Fáil it did in fact deny them seats and the vital few they needed to get a majority. Haughey appeared cursed and in the days following the election went into a black depression. It was left to my father and Ray MacSharry to go out to Kinsealy and pick him off the ground. My father said he was in a pitiful condition, incoherent and emotional. My father told him to get ready for government and that there was now an opportunity to govern as if Fianna Fáil had a majority by playing off the right and the left in the context of the new configuration of sets in Leinster House. My father felt they could defy the Opposition to bring them down. MacSharry was more than anxious to do the right thing by the economy and push the financial adjustments needed to turn Ireland around. Both men felt that this was a great opportunity to do the right thing. MacSharry insisted on his own condition that he be given full freedom in relation to the economy – freedom that is from interference from Haughey. Likewise my father secured full, operational freedom, in relation to the north with a commitment to run with the Anglo-Irish agreement. Haughey was to sit over things and supervise rather than micromanage departments as had been his wont in the recent past.

CHAPTER TWELVE

RECOVERY

Ray MacSharry was to become the best Taoiseach that the country never had. With Haughey back in power he agreed to become Minister for Finance with one important proviso — total independence in the pursuit of his objectives for the economy and the exchequer. He had learnt the hard lesson of dealing with Charlie Haughey in 1981 and 1982 as his party leader switched positions on fiscal rectitude. MacSharry had been Haughey's main campaign manager and advisor right back to the time when he contested for the leadership in 1979. In the wake of the bugging controversy he had kept a low profile and spent a while in the European parliament before running again for his Sligo constituency in 1987. Now he was back and over the next two years he was to impose a financial discipline on his colleagues that earned him the nickname 'Mac the Knife'. He was considered a lot more ruthless than Haughey and very disciplined in his approach. He earned a reputation for consistency with colleagues. They knew he would not back off or seek some sort of shoddy compromise. Des O'Malley would hardly be considered a political fan of MacSharry but even he is generous in his praise about both Haughey and MacSharry in this phase.

MacSharry and Haughey were also greatly helped by the fact that Alan Dukes, now leader of Fine Gael, had decided to issue his 'Tallaght Strategy' which can be briefly explained as a decision to support the government in the Dáil as long as they were implementing measures to bring the public finances back into order. It was a brave decision on the part of Dukes and one for which he got no real electoral reward.

Des O'Malley states:

> *"I would give Haughey – and MacSharry – credit for beginning to tackle the serious deficit problem. Haughey was highly opportunist in opposition up to 1987, opposing all cuts and promising to spend money everywhere; he implemented the correct fiscal policies when in office, even if it was a U-turn of massive proportions."*[57]

There was remarkable unity of purpose within this government that ran from 1987 to 1989. Apart from MacSharry and my father, Haughey was supported by a very able ministerial team, all of whom were loyal and determined to see the business through. Desperate times required desperate remedies. The fact that Fianna Fáil had clearly not won the 1987 general election outright justified their strong action. The fact that they were a minority government that could be pulled down, at any time, meant the government ran a tight ship, with little room for the kind of internal dissent that had characterised Haughey's previous administrations. One of the real heroes of this government was a mild-mannered medical Doctor called Rory O'Hanlon. Though a health professional, he did not flinch from imposing stringent cuts to the Health budget, despite enormous public pressure on him as well as, without doubt, the scorn of his own profession.

---

[57]O'Malley, Desmond, *Conduct Unbecoming – A Memoir*, Gill & Macmillan, 2014, p. 178

The ministers who performed well under Haughey tended to be those who were least afraid of him. He had a notorious tendency to try to bully colleagues. His tantrums were an accepted feature. Murtagh and Joyce wrote well on this back in the 1980s: "He would lose his temper suddenly over something apparently trivial, tossing papers about, slamming down phones and abusing people with foul language."[58] He was, to say the very least of it, a very driven man. That said, few public servants have indicated that they found it difficult to work with him. In fact most of the senior public servants that I met, in my own period in public life, said that they found him to be 'head and shoulders' above others that they had worked for. He had a great mind, read assiduously and mastered any brief that was given to him.

In the early 1980s Haughey had been dismissive of a few things. In the first place was the notion of monetarism, a new economic philosophy espoused by those on the right, the followers of the US Economist Milton Friedman. Thatcher was a big fan of the latter and the economic philosopher Friedrich Hayek. Haughey's default position up until this point had been Keynesian economics. Both in his public life and private life, as things turned out, he was much happier when spending money and priming the economy, as he saw it. Shortly after taking office in 1987 he made a few extraordinary statements indicating he had changed his mind. At a gathering of economists he reportedly threw in "We are all monetarists now". In the 1980s the Dublin bar Doheny & Nesbitt's gave rise to a term the "The Doheny & Nesbitt's School of Economics". Amongst its frequent denizens, apart from civil servants and politicians, was one Colm McCarthy, an at times outspoken critic of Haughey's spendthrift ways. Haughey would often spit out the words 'Doheny & Nesbitt's School' with a sort of derision. McCarthy was a habituee of Doheny & Nesbitt's. In a well-publicised interview Haughey was asked for his

[58]Joyce, Joe and Murtagh, Peter, *The Boss*, Poolbeg Press, 1983

view about economists. His disregard for the profession was obvious and he stated: " When we need an economist we will send for one". Yet, barely months back in office, he appointed Colm McCarthy, arguably his most forensic critic from years past, as the Chief Economic Advisor to the government. McCarthy's role was to guide ministers as to where best to make the spending cuts.

Haughey was a great fan of Seán Lemass. The latter had been one of the first to develop centralised wage agreements with the trade unions. In the 1980s in Ireland there had been some admiration expressed at the way in which Germany had systemised its own commitment to industrial pay restraint through a process of bargaining between the state, the employers and the unions. This gave greater certainty to all players over a longer time horizon than the alternate scenario which essentially meant free collective bargaining on a year-to-year basis. Haughey, with his strong trade union connections, moved to set up a system of national wage agreements. These were later to be termed partnership deals.

In the 1980s, the worry was that Ireland would go down the English road of industrial chaos, frequent disputes and mounting lost productivity days through strikes. Haughey initiated a constructive dialogue with the social partners and they agreed to pay restraint. These national pay agreements, multiannual in their scope, soon became an essential part of the Irish economic recovery. The consensus approach to wages and conditions was soon widened to cover wider economic policy and legislation. Though this process was to become the target of intense criticism in the later boom years of the 1990s it certainly contributed industrial peace, co-operation and consensus at a time when the country really needed this. Bertie Ahern, whom Haughey appointed as Minister for Labour, would have carved out his political reputation as a negotiator because of this process initiated by Haughey. It was after Ahern had saved Haughey's reputation in one particular negotiation that Haughey famously described him as; "the most skilful, the most devious, the most cunning of them all".

The harsh medicine on the economy was showing signs of working. Quite early in Haughey's new administration, German investors decided that Ireland was now a different place and that the Irish government was serious in tackling its economic difficulties. My father, through his friendship with the German Foreign Minister Hans-Dietrich Genscher, had played a small role in convincing the German investment community to take a different view of Ireland. The German investment in Irish government-issued bonds put a strong floor under Ireland and was soon a talking point in the wider global investment community.

Prior to his arrival in power in 1987, Haughey had been approached by Dermot Desmond, then less famous, but the owner of NCB Stockbrokers, a relatively recent and go-getting firm on the Dublin scene. Desmond had an idea of creating a hub for financial services in Dublin. He had gone to the bother of spending £35,000 of his own money on a feasibility study for his plans. The nub of the plan was to leverage off Dublin's proximity to London by creating niche or complementary services to those available in the British capital. It was way beyond most people's understanding or imaginative range at the time. Desmond had pitched his idea past both Ruairi Quinn and Garret FitzGerald in the previous government but had got nowhere. Haughey seized on Desmond's idea and instructed his officials to clear the obstacles to it. In the 1987 election Haughey went to the bother of producing a glamorous brochure outlining his plans for financial services in a separate document to the formal election manifesto. Once in government, Haughey also instructed the agencies to put people on it and develop Desmond's ideas further. It was a telling and illustrative example of how Haughey differed from his predecessors. In economic terms, one of Haughey's great strengths was that he was development-minded. He knew and understood how to move projects forward in an efficient manner. He was not afraid to think big and back big projects. He attracted to himself powerful and talented people within the civil service who were more than ready to push forward his plans. In his first term as Taoiseach, Pádraig Ó hAnnracháin and Brendan O'Donnell were key drivers. Later on Padraig O hUiginn was to make concrete his plans for the Irish Financial Services Centre by pushing it through the system.

The contribution made by the Irish Financial Services Centre to economic recovery and investment was enormous. First of all, as international banks established there, they poured millions in taxes into what was then a quite distressed exchequer. The taxes paid by these companies were allowing the state to consider modest expansions in other lines of spending. From an investment perspective, as large investment and banking institutions established offices in Dublin, a wide message of confidence was sent around the world about the Irish economy. The high-rise buildings and high occupancy soon became symbols in their own rights of Irish economic recovery.

The Dockside area where the Financial Services Centre is located, was, for the entirety of my upbringing, a run down place, a location of urban blight and an embarrassment to the city of Dublin. Today in excess of 35,000 are employed in the IFSC. Many of the young people employed there have the opportunity of a first job in the industry, an opportunity that was simply not there for the generation I was part of when I graduated from UCD in 1984.

From 1987 onwards, because of continuing high unemployment, Haughey put a huge emphasis on improving the country's tourist visitor figures. In government, Fianna Fáil challenged the natural monopoly that Aer Lingus, the national airline, enjoyed on the London route. Ryanair were first licenced to operate this route in competition to Aer Lingus during the Haughey government. It was a difficult decision to make given the entrenched monopoly interests at Dublin Airport and in Aer Lingus. In a subsequent interview with the state broadcaster RTÉ, the then Minister for Transport and Tourism Séamus Brennan was harried on air with claims that his government was showing favouritism to Ryanair. The air fares came tumbling down and this route is now one of the busiest and most valuable routes in the world.

The government had set some very ambitious targets around tourist visitor numbers. Tax incentives were put in place to create more bedspaces in Dublin. Haughey, at a personal level, as Taoiseach supervised and oversaw the transformation of Temple Bar into a trendy, as opposed to run-down, location that could absorb the weekend visitors that we were now as a country trying to accommodate. Haughey and the then Secretary of the Government, Paddy Teahon, put their weight behind this project. Nowadays it is an indispensable part of the offer that Dublin City makes to visitors. On one occasion, Haughey called a press conference to update people on the progress on the project. Only three journalists attended; myself, George Lee, then with the *Sunday Business Post* and Frank McDonald, Environment Correspondent of the *Irish Times*. The tension between McDonald and Haughey was palpable. McDonald's book *The Destruction of Dublin* points the finger of blame for the decline of Georgian Dublin at a lot of Haughey's developer friends from the 1960s. Haughey and McDonald were courteous but there was a needle being used on both sides of the conversation.

Haughey, despite his critics who saw him as permanently wed to the interests of developers, showed a huge interest in heritage and restoration. In this, his last spell as

Taoiseach, he turned the old Royal Hospital in Kilmainham into the location for the Irish Museum of Modern Art and at the same time funded the huge re-development of the National Gallery and the addition of its new, more modern, expansion. He, naturally enough given his position, took a huge personal interest in the restoration of the Taoiseach's new, palatial, offices on Merrion Street. When it was finished he personally guided groups of journalists through the building, including a visit to his own opulent, oak-lined, office. He was charm personified as he brought journalists' attention to particular paintings, objets d'art and sculpture pieces that decorated the place. Some were so surprised at the tasteful job that they had seen that they asked who were the outside consultants, presuming there were foreign consultants involved. Haughey indicated to Angela Rolfe, the supervising architect, who took great pride in pointing out it was entirely the work of the Office of Public Works. It is a hugely impressive place and one that has an impact on foreign dignitaries.

Haughey, in this period, was performing at a very high level. On the wider European stage, along with my father, he was cultivating relationships with political leaders. He made a strong alliance with French President François Mitterrand, German Chancellor Helmut Kohl and the President of the European Commission Jacques Delors. In this period Ireland benefitted disproportionately from European Union funding, relative to countries that were far poorer than we were and could arguably have deserved to get more than we did. Our foreign policy was carefully designed to be supportive of the aims and objectives of the European Commission. Our 'Communautaire' approach meant we got the breaks when we needed them from the Brussels administration. In fairness, FitzGerald had also done a very good job in this respect. We also got good jobs when it came to appointments at the European Commission. Ray MacSharry got the hugely important agriculture brief when Ireland needed someone there to ensure that the EU's reform plans were not hostile to Ireland.

Haughey's relationship with the press was always characterised as mutually hostile. The leadership heaves against him in the middle 1980s only made the relationship worse. The whole scene changed a lot when he came into government in 1987. P.J. Mara was set to become almost as well-known as Haughey himself. He seemed to be able to soothe the frayed nerves of the media when it came to Haughey. As a journalist I dealt with him, pretty much, on a daily basis. He had what every journalist wanted from a Government Press Secretary – direct personal access to the levers of power and his boss. Like Bernard Ingham, whom I worked with as a Political Correspondent at the Palace of Westminster, he had unique access to the head of government. He and Haughey were friends, which made a big difference. P.J., with no prior experience in this area, wined and dined the press, winning their confidence but more importantly earning their trust. P.J. Mara had that same ability as his eponymous Boss – the capability to be both lethal and amusing from one minute to the next. Opinion polls showed Haughey was riding on a crest of a wave.

Pride it seems, in relation to Haughey, came before a fall. In early 1989, Haughey had just returned from a state visit to Japan to learn that the government had been defeated in the Dáil over compensation payments to haemophiliacs who had contracted AIDS through blood transfusions. It was a minor issue, in the run of things, but Haughey wanted to call an election, perhaps influenced by the fact that Fianna Fáil had been getting 50% approval levels over the previous year. He was clearly irritated by the Dáil defeat, jet lagged from his visit to Japan and probably pumped up with a sense of importance because of the deference and courtesy he received from his Japanese hosts. My father was sick at the time and soon to be bound for the States to have a liver transplant. Haughey came to see him in the Mater hospital. My father advised against holding an election. Pádraig Flynn and Ray Burke, who were always a bit too bullish for most people's liking, were the two ministers who were urging Haughey to go to the country. MacSharry was now gone to Europe as Commissioner and my father out of the loop through illness. Wiser heads should have prevailed but did not.

My father's condition had deteriorated to the point that his medical advisors in Ireland were recommending he go to the Mayo Clinic, in the States, for a liver transplant. It was a worrying time for the family. The fact that there would now be an election brought additional pressures. I came back from London, where I lived, to help out with the campaign. My father had been assured that the clinic in the States offered him the best chance of survival, subject of course to their being a suitable organ available. It was a nerve-wracking time for Mum, who had chosen to accompany my father to the US. Haughey had been hugely supportive of my father as his condition got worse. Some had questioned whether he should have stayed on in government but Haughey wanted him to remain in his position. When Haughey heard that my father needed the liver transplant he immediately organised people to raise the funds to pay for the treatment, hospital stay in the US and the operation itself. He knew my parents could not have afforded this treatment. Haughey instructed the party's election fundraiser Paul Kavanagh to also raise money to defray the cost of my father's medical expenses. Separate to this, Peter Hanley, a personal friend of my father's, was also involved in raising funds to help with the costs. Kavanagh and Peter Hanley co-ordinated with each other as to who they were making contact with. It is also clear from the Tribunal of Inquiry into his finances, which reported in 2006, that Haughey also brought influence to bear so that the VHI board made a quick decision in relation to how much they would contribute to the patient costs.

As a family we have no complaint about how Haughey treated my father at this time. In fact he showed enormous care and concern for my father. According to his Personal Assistant Catherine Butler he broke down in tears when he heard that my father would die if he did not have a successful transplant.[59] He did not want to see him die and made great efforts to ensure that my father did not have to worry about the cost of the treatment he required in the US. Many years later the whole issue of Haughey's finances came under intense scrutiny. When the Moriarty Tribunal concluded its investigations into the matter it concluded that of the £270,000 raised for the purpose of my father's operation no more than £70,000 ended up being spent on his medical care. It also stated that one £20,000 donation was quietly appropriated by Haughey and attempts made to conceal the transaction. This caused enormous damage to Haughey's reputation with the public, although by the time it came out, he was in retirement. The fact that he had re-allocated some of the money raised for my father's medical treatment was instanced as another, very glaring example, of what a terrible character he was.

By 2006 when the Moriarty report came out I was, at the time myself, a junior minister in the government in an important portfolio. At the time Bertie Ahern relied on my skills for television and media appearances generally. I was deemed to be a good man to send on when things were a little difficult for the government. In other words I could handle myself. Bertie's Special Advisor Mandy Johnston rang me up. The Taoiseach wanted someone to go on *Prime Time*, RTÉ's current affairs show, that night to set out the government's line on the Moriarty Tribunal. Mandy said she and the Taoiseach both understood if I did <u>not want to go</u> on, given the content in the report about my

[59]Quoted in RTÉ Documentary Series *'Haughey'*, Mint Productions, 2005

father's operation, so she added, "It's totally up to you". I said I would get back to her. I spoke to my Mum to clarify her thoughts on the matter and rang Mandy back. I felt that there was no point in me being in the government if I could not go on, in all occasions and circumstances, and account for myself and my presence in the government. On the show itself Miriam O'Callaghan spent the early part of the discussion on Haughey and how damaging the whole thing was. I made the point that thankfully, this kind of money, could never again be given to a politician in the state because of the legislation we had passed to control and regulate the amounts and donations that those in politics could receive. In relation to the money raised for my father's operation I pointed out that Mr Haughey had been quite kind to my father at that time. When grilled on the money taken from the fund I simply replied that we, as a family, were not party to this effort and that our only concern was that my father would get healthy again. I also tried to make the point that this was not our money and that if there were problems, whereby donors who had given money felt aggrieved, they should take legal or other steps to retrieve their money.

Haughey, to my mind, and that of my mother, had been good to my father during that terrible time in his life. I was not going to join the chorus of anger about the money and how it had been allocated once Haughey and his people discovered there was in fact a surplus to what was required. None of the family were told about who had actually donated the funds, nor was there a need to. Later on, after his return from the US, my father may have inquired from Peter Hanley and Paul Kavanagh as to the identity of the donors so as to thank them. In some cases he may have done so because they had volunteered that they had given when they met him at some function or other. It seems to me that the appropriate thing for Haughey to do would have been to have returned the surplus amounts to the individual donors.

However this may have been too complicated for him, as is clear from the Tribunal report, that some donors were splitting their donations between the party's election fund and my father's operation. Having read about the period it seems that similar issues arose with regard to how Haughey handled the Leader's Allowance fund over the years – that is the fund whereby the Dáil votes money to assist a party leader to run his party operation in opposition.

On his return from the United States my father was given a very emotional greeting in the Dáil. He had his operation and returned in time to cast his vote and nominate Charlie Haughey to be the next Taoiseach. The 1989 election had been a disaster and as predicted by my father support for Fianna Fáil had dropped consistently, once the election was called. The opinion poll ratings the party had been receiving had been conditional on the party continuing to do a good job. By calling the election Fianna Fáil were creating instability and doubt in the voter's mind. The public could not understand why an election was needed, a point made very well by John Bruton in the election's aftermath. Haughey was in an even tighter spot than in 1987 when it came to forming a government. After a period when it became obvious that nobody could actually form a government, the prospect of another general election became a possibility. Haughey decided to open discussions with his arch-rival Desmond O'Malley, whose party the Progressive Democrats had six seats, compared to their previous 14, which was enough to give Haughey a majority in the Dáil.

"When the PDs would settle for nothing less than full coalition, Haughey circumvented considerable Opposition within Fianna Fáil ('Only myself could have done it,' he boasted) and concluded a deal giving the PDs two cabinet positions and a Junior Ministry."[60]

[60]Maume, Patrick, *Monograph on Haughey*, Royal Irish Academy, Dictionary of Irish Biography

Haughey, in making the deal with the Progressive Democrats was annoying a good number of his own deputies. There was still a great deal of resentment towards them within the party ranks. Fianna Fáil, since it had been founded in 1926, had never formed a coalition government. In fact the party made this one of its unique selling points over the years. They would frequently push the line to voters that coalition governments were inherently unstable and bad for the country. It was a somewhat superficial line to use but some of the party activists had taken it to heart. In a democracy all sorts of combinations are required and the only way for other parties to keep Fianna Fáil out of power over the years was to form coalitions. Members of Haughey's own cabinet took great exception to what had been done. Máire Geoghegan-Quinn complained it "was simply being done to satisfy the leader's desire for power". Albert Reynolds and Bertie Ahern had been formally tasked to negotiate with Bobby Molloy and Pat Cox of the Progressive Democrats. The harder the deal they tried to strike the less interested the PDs became. Both Reynolds and Ahern had an uneasy feeling about the whole thing and felt a little bit used when it emerged that Haughey had gone behind their backs to negotiate directly with O'Malley and the PDs. It made Albert Reynolds and Ahern look foolish, all the more so in Reynolds' case, as he was now Haughey' Minister for Finance. Pádraig Flynn, who had urged Haughey to have an election in 1989 was now also furious. He attacked Haughey, much to the surprise of his colleagues, later declaring that everyone was against coalition "the National Executive, the Parliamentary Party and the grassroots have indicated this is a core value which we must preserve."[61]

Albert Reynolds was now, increasingly seen within the party, as the obvious challenger to replace Haughey. In

---

[61]Dwyer, T.Ryle, *Haughey's Thirty Years of Controversy*, Mercier Press, 1992, p. 140

less than two and a half years Haughey would be gone as Taoiseach. People like Albert Reynolds, Pádraig Flynn and Máire Geoghegan-Quinn would be seeking to move him on. Haughey, in 1989, had paid unbeknownst to himself a very high price for his ambition to remain in power. It is noteworthy that the people who were now devoted to taking him out were not the dissident types of old. The people who were now coming after him were precisely the people who had put Jack Lynch out of his job and Haughey in position. They were not members of the party who could be depicted as disloyal or in some way never accepting of his rule. They were the people who had kept him in office. In the meantime Ireland was to play host to the Presidency of the European Union in the first part of 1990. It was an important opportunity for Ireland and for Haughey. Haughey grabbed the opportunity with both hands. He excelled in the role and was helped by the fact that the Berlin Wall had come down. Instead of the usual single summit Ireland had to host two meetings of European leaders at Dublin Castle. The second summit was to organise Europe's assistance for the new countries of Eastern Europe who had just recently been liberated from Soviet control.

Haughey was a perfectionist when it came to looking after his European Head of State colleagues. The recently refurbished Dublin Castle buildings made it possible to host these large meetings conveniently in one location. I was a journalist covering these events. British and foreign colleagues were surprised at the sophistication and efficiency of the Irish operation. There was a gift pack for all of the visiting journalists which included Irish Whiskey, a CD of Irish music and a vacuum packed side of Irish smoked salmon. The whole thing ran very smoothly and one of the big summits coincided with Ireland's World Cup campaign. I was in this press briefing being held by Haughey as the cliffhanger penalty shoot out was occurring to decide whether Ireland or Romania would go through. Tommy

Gorman, the RTÉ Correspondent, shouted over Haughey: "If David O'Leary gets the next one we're through". The assembled world press corps thought Gorman a little insolent as Gorman received this piece of information through his earpiece. Haughey stood up from his seat and barked out the order, while pointing at a nearby television, "Will someone turn it on". The screen flashed up as O'Leary was taking his back steps before striking the penalty kick in the net. Haughey was ecstatic, cupping his two hands in the air, and marched straight past the assembled journalists into the courtyard of Dublin Castle to do a live interview with RTÉ to congratulate the Irish soccer team. Haughey never missed a chance for positive publicity, particularly when there was an open goal there in front of him.

The Presidency of the European Union was to be his last really comfortable period in public office. He was now at the beginning of the end to his leadership. The friends he had made at a European level ensured that Ireland got significant funding from the European Union's regional and infrastructural funds. When David O'Leary put the goal in the net the whole country went mad. Around the city and outside the walls of Dublin Castle one could hear the endless chant of: "Óle, Óle, Óle" the song that had become the anthem of Irish supporters as Jack Charlton's team made their steady progress through the world cup competition. The bars and pubs were crammed with people. People were dancing on the roofs of cars, horns blaring, hugs all round. Ireland wanted to party, things were going well. The soccer team became emblematic of the progress the country was making. There was a real sense that the country had turned the corner and would never look back. As the Political Scientist Tom Garvin has acknowledged, historians will give credit to Haughey for starting the Irish economic miracle that took root in the late 1990s. [62]

---

[62]As quoted in RTÉ, Mint Productions Documentary on Haughey, 2005

CHAPTER THIRTEEN

PRESIDENTIAL ELECTION

An uneasy peace had settled in Fianna Fáil in the aftermath of the ground-breaking decision by Haughey to be the first leader of his party to formally involve Fianna Fáil in a coalition with another party. The talk of a core value being breached had begun to die down and most observers felt that the Fianna Fáil/Progressive Democrat coalition was doing quite a good job, my father included.

My father had said some very critical things over the years about the Progressive Democrats but now as Tánaiste and Minister for Defence he was prepared to be generous about them. My father was not among those, like Pádraig Flynn, who believed that single party government was some sort of 'core value' of the party. Like many others he had come to the conclusion that the days of actually winning overall majorities was a thing of the past. My father also took the view that most of the heavy lifting, in terms of correcting the public finances, had already been done by the minority government that had preceded the Fianna Fáil/Progressive Democrat coalition. In terms of his own situation, he was content to be in the Department of Defence. He set about resolving the problems within the army over the representative associations and the bad blood that had been created over this issue.

Speculation was growing within the party and within the media about who would succeed Patrick Hillery as president of Ireland. Within government P.J. Mara and Charlie McCreevy became advocates of the idea that my father should be the party nominee for the presidency. My father was not averse to the idea and discussed it in depth with both men. His popularity at a national level had been clearly demonstrated by the public reaction to his liver transplant operation and subsequent return to work in the Dáil and in the government. His eventual run for the presidency would not be without controversy.

Over the years my father had always taken the view that it was good to be helpful to those doing doctoral or other types of academic theses on issues relating to his role in public life. One such researcher from UCD called Jim Duffy made a request and my father obliged with an interview in May of 1990. Under usual circumstances, these interviews are deemed to be confidential and only to be used for the purposes of research. Duffy was doing an M.A. thesis on the Presidency. Amongst other things Duffy wanted to know a little more about the events of 1982 when on the occasion of the fall of Garret FitzGerald's government, Haughey had wanted to remind the then President, Patrick Hillery, that it was possible not to have an election and wished to seek to establish if he could form a government without an election.

There was nothing too controversial in what my father told Duffy. However one casual claim, made by my father, was to come back to haunt him during his own presidential campaign and cost him the Presidency. What my father told Duffy was unusual, in that he not only confirmed he made phone calls to President Hillery back in 1982, but that he had actually spoken to the President. Duffy used the interview material he had gathered from my father. He told Fine Gael activists and friends about the contents of the interview. During the election campaign itself, when confronted on the issue, my father simply denied on television that he had made any of the phone calls. His accuser on the TV programme was Garret FitzGerald, the former Taoiseach. The issue became a huge public controversy. My father had denied making the calls but then Jim Duffy was persuaded by the *Irish Times* to play his taped interview to a press pack who were jumping all over the issue. Des O'Malley stated in an interview on RTÉ that, "Mr Lenihan has given two diametrically opposed accounts of what happened and they can't both be true".

My father had been on heavy medication at the time of giving the interview to Duffy. The medication was to prevent his body from rejecting his new liver. In the context of the campaign, he felt it would only worsen things for him if he introduced that key fact. The media at this stage were ready for a full pack hunt and the issue of his health would only add further controversy to an already difficult campaign. Haughey was now in a very difficult situation, as was of course, my father. Haughey had been the one to initiate the attempted contacts with President Hillery and he did not want to be drawn into the maelstrom of controversy. His coalition partners the Progressive Democrats, though ostensibly neutral in the Presidential election, were hopping up and down indicating their unhappiness. They were now a very small party of six and very much influenced by media opinion. According to O'Malley,

"We had formally remained outside the election, although there was considerable support in the party for Mary Robinson's candidacy. Lenihan's contradictory statements on whether or not he had put pressure on President Hillery not to dissolve the Dáil

in early 1982 placed us in a difficult situation. It was not a problem we made but it was a very real problem. Letters of resignation were prepared; we put the party on an election footing. But Haughey was not keen to face the electorate, and when Lenihan refused to resign he was duly sacked."[63]

Prior to sacking my father, Haughey had put in place relentless behind-the-scenes pressure to get my father to resign. Haughey was living in fear of an election and afraid to face down the Progressive Democrats who were urging him to get my father to resign. Meanwhile my father formed the view, on advice from family and friends, that to resign would render his prospects in the Presidential election impossible. He also felt that the particular controversy, albeit of his own making, cast no reflection on him as a Presidential candidate or indeed in his role as Tánaiste and Minister for Defence. My father continued with his campaign. He was then summoned to Kinsealy to meet Haughey, where we duly arrived by helicopter. He went in to speak with him while his campaign road manager Michael Dawson, my brother and I waited in an adjacent room. Haughey told my father that he should resign as it would be good for his campaign and that Des O'Malley would congratulate him on his decision. This latter element seemed to us ridiculous. My father asked us what we thought. Dawson said resignation would sink the campaign. We all agreed with him. Later, in the Dáil, more of my father's colleagues met with him and presumably on instructions from Haughey urged him to resign. There was an air of desperation to all of their efforts. The only minister who was quite cool in his advice was Albert Reynolds who said my father should not resign and that the pressure should be put back on the PDs.

We took to the helicopter again and resumed campaigning in the midlands. Haughey had handed my father a draft

[63]O'Malley, Desmond, *Conduct Unbecoming – A Memoir*, Gill & Macmillan, 2014, p. 188

letter of resignation that was pathetic. The tone of it read like a political suicide note. It was designed to take all blame for the Hillery affair away from Haughey. The opposition had a 'No Confidence' motion ready to be debated in the Dáil the next day, a deadline that Haughey and the PDs were working against. Still on the campaign trail, my mother read the would-be resignation letter at the back of the campaign bus. Having read it once, she tore it to pieces, telling my father we would have no more to do with that. Meanwhile, the pressure from Haughey was redoubling by the hour. Pádraig Flynn and Bertie Ahern were sent down to the Athlone election rally to get my father to re-consider. The crowd knew why they were there and started chanting "No resignation". They were so scared by what they saw, they retired to an upstairs room in the hotel. There were so many supporters, you could not move within the hotel and huge numbers crowded outside on the street. Bertie Ahern was the Director of the Presidential election and was in a bit of a quandary.

The following day, Haughey was putting on more pressure in an effort to bring my father back to Dublin so that he could be cajoled by colleagues. Staying in the home of some family friends, my father decided to sleep on it and see how the land lay the following morning.

In Dublin, Haughey kept complaining to TDs and anyone who would listen to him that he could not make contact with my father. He was creating the impression that my father was ignoring him. Haughey could easily have called my father. He had all of the phone numbers for my father, the campaign staff and, of course, Bertie Ahern. Haughey was creating a smokescreen for himself and at the same time trying, one last time, to secure my father's resignation before the crucial Dáil vote.

My father spent the hours before the vote in the home of a friend in Rathgar. A family friend came to the house and asked that we meet with Des O'Malley. My father was not inclined to do that. Over the phone, he confirmed to the Taoiseach that he was not going to resign. Shortly afterwards, two army motorcycle riders arrived out to the house, one with a letter in his leather dispatch bag which he handed to my father. It was a letter from the Taoiseach terminating his appointment as Tánaiste and Minister for Defence.[64]

My father drove to Leinster House to vote confidence in the government. There was a strange atmosphere in Leinster House. Few could believe that my father had actually been sacked. The confidence debate itself was a dramatic affair. It was a bitter debate and Dick Spring made a speech, which many took objection to, the key piece of which read as follows:

"This debate is not about Brian Lenihan when it is all boiled down. This debate, essentially, is about the evil spirit that controls one political party in this Republic, and it is about the way in which that spirit has begun to corrupt the entire political system in our country. This is a debate about greed for office, about disregard for the truth and about contempt for political standards. It is a debate about the way in which a once great party has been brought to its knees by the grasping acquisitiveness of its leader. It is ultimately a debate about the cancer that is eating away at our body politic – and the virus which caused that cancer, An Taoiseach, Charles J. Haughey."

The speech was rather like the speech made back in 1979 by Garret FitzGerald about Haughey's flawed pedigree. It demonstrated, once again, the toxic nature of Haughey when it came to his opponents. My father met Haughey after the Dáil vote and Haughey tried to mollify him. My <u>father, for his</u> part, was matter-of-fact in his replies. There

[64]See Appendix I, Letter from Charles Haughey to Brian Lenihan Senior, 31 October 1990

was a discernible parting of the ways. My father then went to face the media at a press conference. He then pushed on with his Presidential campaign.

The reaction to my father's dismissal was extraordinary. It was as if by facing down Haughey in his request for his resignation, my father had mobilised the whole country. He was mobbed on the campaign trail. It was also clear in the opinion polls, where his ratings bounced back, whereas prior to the sacking they had slumped. Lorna Reid, a respected political reporter with the *Irish Independent,* wrote about witnessing 'a squalid political mugging'. Public sympathy was with my father. Few, if anybody, quite understood how things had become so serious that it had merited his sacking from government. There was a populist frenzy to the late period of the campaign. Into this tinderbox of public excitement stepped Pádraig Flynn. In the words of T. Ryle Dwyer,

"Lenihan's dismissal provoked a strong reaction from the grassroots of the Party and a great wave of support for him. He began to regain lost ground by leaps and bounds and might even have turned about the election had it not been for some unfortunate remarks by Pádraig Flynn during a radio programme on which he seemed to question Mary Robinson's suitability as a wife and mother. That put paid to whatever chance Lenihan had."[65]

The comments by Flynn were deemed to have been offensive to women generally and not just Mary Robinson. The sense of outrage was added to, on the actual programme itself, when another panelist, Michael McDowell, expressed indignation at what had been said. Sympathy, in the public mind, was being displaced from Lenihan to Robinson.

After the election was over, my father insisted that his friendship with Haughey had been on a professional level.

---

[65]Dwyer, T. Ryle, *Haughey's Thirty Years of Controversy*, Mercier Press, 1992, p. 151

At home he did become a little more frank about him. I encouraged my father to write a book about the events of the Presidential election. He was a little bit reluctant at first. His natural inclination was not to upset people and keep the door open for a potential political return. Eventually he relented and decided to write a book about what had happened during the presidential campaign. I helped him with the book but struggled with his reticence on a number of subjects. He did, though, confide in me that one of the reasons he had chosen to stand for the Presidency was to exit from Haughey's government. He told me that he had seen things that made him wary of being in the government. Things he felt were about to, or could easily, collapse. Haughey, he told me, had become "very venal" in this his last period as Taoiseach. It was clear to him that Haughey was now cashing in on the success he had made of the economy. My father suspected that there was a considerable amount of money being pocketed by Haughey for his own ends. My father's instinct was that in these, Haughey's final years in office, discretion had been thrown to the four winds. As always with Haughey, down the years, this was often hard to detect. My father had been a very good friend to Haughey over the years and for the most part Haughey had reciprocated that friendship. The Presidential election was the exception. My father did not say these things out of a sense of anger but rather a significant concern he had that this might, at some point, crash in on the party and damage it substantially. My father would pass away before the truth about Haughey's finances came flooding into the public gaze.

Some years previous to all this, in the 1980s, my father was drawn to comment, by myself and my brother Brian, about a statement Haughey had made to the *Sunday Press*. It was before his return to government in 1987 and out of the blue, Haughey had issued a press statement, exclusively carried by the *Sunday Press*, where he seemed to be calling for the nationalisation of the banks. It was a

Sunday and we were sitting around the front room of our home, pouring over the newspapers. I tackled Dad on the statement, being a little left wing, complementing Haughey on his radicalism. My brother Brian came in on a right wing tack, talking about the statement as if it were economic lunacy. My father, deeply engrossed behind his newspaper, refused initially to respond to our conversational prompts. Eventually he calmed my brother down by baldly stating: "He [Haughey] is probably under pressure from his bank". I suspect my father did not know at that stage how close he was to the actual truth of the situation facing Haughey. Haughey, in fact, as we now know from the Tribunal of Inquiry into his affairs, was in 1987, as in 1979, living well beyond his means and owed a substantial sum of money that he was under pressure to repay. This was when Ben Dunne stepped in and offered him a million pounds.

Haughey's position as leader of Fianna Fáil was to come under significantly more pressure following the Presidential election. In fact, even before it had started, there were some significant straws in the wind that forces within the parliamentary party were becoming organised in this respect. Seán Power, a backbencher, who would eventually put down a motion calling on Haughey to resign, had indicated to Haughey fairly bluntly on the day of my father's sacking what would happen when the Progressive Democrats came looking for his (Haughey's) head on a plate. There was a general sense that the Progressive Democrats had been given many more concessions than they deserved. When Haughey went behind the backs of his cabinet colleagues to conclude the negotiations with the PDs he had significantly insulted some of his colleagues. At one point he told his interlocutors that his backbench TDs were more receptive to the coalition than his cabinet, who he described as "gobshites". Haughey, in the wake of the Presidential debacle, was beginning to realise that some of his colleagues, Albert Reynolds in particular, were out to take his job from him.

Albert Reynolds, from his perspective, was getting anxious to move Haughey on. In his interview with the Mint Productions series on Haughey for RTÉ some years later, Reynolds was moved to tears with sheer emotion as he remembered how he became convinced that he would have to move against Haughey; "I wouldn't be where I am but for him," he states. Haughey and his innermost advisors were moving their propaganda line out in advance of any threat from Albert. Reynolds and his friends in the party were being disparaged as being part of the "Country & Western" wing of the party. The subliminal message was that Reynolds and his gang were a bunch of provincial hicks compared to the metropolitan and urbane values that Haughey's discerning crew upheld. This smear was useful for Haughey, for defence purposes, but ultimately damaging to the Fianna Fáil party interests. Some of Haughey's aides had assisted the producers of *Eat the Peach*, a celebrated movie in this period, which featured a white-suited character that was modelled on Reynolds.

My father, now a backbench TD for the first time in his life, began to think about party matters and how he could contribute to them in his new role. For years he had been a Joint Honorary Secretary. Now people were urging him to consider running for the party leadership at the forthcoming Ard Fhéis. In purely technical terms, the party leadership, or Presidency of the Party, is chosen at the Ard Fhéis by the ordinary delegate membership. Never in the history of the party has there been a challenge. Normally the Ard Fhéis acts as the rubber stamp for the leadership selection made by the parliamentary party. Members of the party were now suggesting that he be nominated for this position and thus separate the party leadership from the person who was the party's nominee to hold the position of Taoiseach. My father's constituency party even went so far as to nominate him to contest the position, such was the bad feeling over the Presidential election. My father ultimately rejected the idea, though he did concede privately that such an idea of separating the two roles was a good one, in the era of coalition, as a way of protecting the party organisation from its role in government. My father normally did the warm up speech before Haughey's appearance on the rostrum to give his party leader's address. In the wake of the Presidential election debacle this duty fell to Máire Geoghegan-Quinn to perform.

Geoghegan-Quinn, a formidable operator, made a speech that referred to the Haughey era in elegiac terms. She summoned up the memories, the achievements and the qualities of Mr Haughey himself. On the surface it appeared to be the standard invocation for a roaring ovation. However it was a speech of huge subtlety that placed the Haughey era in a historical context. In other words, when listened to carefully, the clear implication was that the Haughey era was now at, or at the very least was nearing, its natural end. Plenty of people got the hint and those close advisors to Haughey who saw it as their job to watch these things were privately furious.

Meanwhile, as noted by Patrick Maume, "A surreal fin de régime atmosphere" was allowed to develop not least because of "the popular RTÉ satirical radio program *Scrap Saturday*, which regularly featured impressions by Dermot Morgan of an autocratic 'Boss' as an absurd and toothless ogre breathing an obsequious P.J. Mara and clinging to preposterously outdated pretensions to sophistication."[66]

The *Scrap Saturday* programme was becoming compelling listening for everyone who had an interest in politics. Dermot Morgan, the comedian, had caught Haughey and his mannerisms. He also ranged over Haughey's entire cabinet, making a particularly biting cut at Pádraig Flynn. The caricature created felt real and it was very funny. At a more serious level, this pantomime approach to Haughey and his regime was corrosive. It caricatured his stock responses, his tendency towards the instant denial, and his

[66] Maume, Patrick, Royal Irish Academy, *Dictionary of Irish Biography*

sonorous tones. It meant that when he faced real problems in the year of the scandals that were about to follow, people were somewhat wise to his ways of denying involvement. When he reached for his stock repertoire of denial, evasion or denunciation it was simply not believed. Haughey had ceased to be a character and was now a caricature.

There were other straws in the wind that were beginning to make people uncomfortable with Haughey. When he came back into government in 1987, Haughey had looked for business champions to push key sectors forward. Dermot Desmond had championed the financial services sector. When it came to the beef industry, he looked to Larry Goodman. The TELESIS report had suggested that the industry should be consolidated from its then position of having a multiplicity of small producers who did not have the ability to scale at an international level. The government and the banks looked to Goodman as the person best placed to do this. In a short period of time he became not just the biggest operator in Ireland but in Europe. Although Goodman got relatively favourable treatment from the FitzGerald government, allegations of favouritism towards him intensified when Haughey came to power. The Labour Party, the Workers Party and the Progressive Democrats, when in opposition, were raising the matter in the Dáil.

In May 1991, the British television station ITV, through its flagship *World in Action* programme, broadcast a series of allegations of malpractice, and of official, as well as political, collusion with the Goodman companies. Haughey when in government on his own had refused to establish a judicial inquiry into the matter despite opposition calls to do so. Now he was in a different position. The PDs, who had called for this inquiry before, were now in government with Haughey. On the day of the Dáil debate on the *World in Action* allegation, I was a reporter in the Press Gallery. Michael O'Kennedy stood up and delivered a script, which had been circulated beforehand. The speech was a staunch defence of the Goodman companies and made no reference to a judicial inquiry. While he was speaking, a colleague gave him a hurried, hand-written note. O'Kennedy climbed down and finished his speech by announcing a public inquiry into the beef industry, which became known as the Goodman Inquiry. Behind the scenes, Haughey had caved in to the demand from the Progressive Democrats. O'Kennedy was an experienced and senior figure. I felt sorry for him that day. He had been made a fool of by his own Taoiseach.

When the Beef Tribunal opened in Dublin Castle, few could have forecast that this one Tribunal would contribute to the departure of a Taoiseach, the collapse of the subsequent Fianna Fáil-PD coalition under Albert Reynolds and then the Fianna Fáil-Labour coalition. On the opening day of the Tribunal a veritable circus of media, PR handlers, lawyers and commentators were gathered expectantly for a feast. Mr Justice Liam Hamilton was the Tribunal Chairman. I had become friends with him down in the Four Courts while covering cases there. I smoked at the time and so did he. He often adjourned his court to grab a cigarette break. One day during the first week, he was gasping for a cigarette, not surprisingly, given the length of the opening submissions. He adjourned mid morning, and as he swept into a room to the side he motioned to me to follow. A journalist colleague, and fellow smoker joined us. We sat on the tea chests containing the massive amount of legal documentation relating to the inquiry, puffing our cigarettes and exchanging views. Hamilton was renowned for pushing barristers to cut down on lengthy submissions. He ran his courtroom in a speedy fashion. The prospect of doing this on the Beef Tribunal, he muttered, was 'daunting'. We respected him a great deal and my colleague was an old school journalist. Hamilton described the Tribunal as a 'ball of political smoke'. He was right but none of us realised how difficult it would all become. Eventually, almost every politician who had made a comment or allegation about

Goodman and his companies would be called before the Tribunal. Every few days my friend and I would dash into the side room to have a smoke with him. Hamilton was desperately worried the whole thing would wreck his legal reputation as a judge. He was originally a member of the Labour Party but was perceived in political circles as very impartial when it came to his role as a judge. Happily for Hamilton, he went on to become Chief Justice. He was one decent man.

The Beef Tribunal became intensely political. The Labour Party and Workers Party had Haughey as their target. O'Malley was focused on Haughey and Reynolds, where he had significant reservations about their actions. Haughey, for his part, was trying to dump all the blame on Reynolds, whose status as threat to him had been upgraded from potential to actual. Reynolds was more than aware that the longer that Haughey lasted, the worse his position would get at the Tribunal. The Beef Tribunal had started a countdown clock for Haughey's departure. Haughey needed to have Reynolds shoulder the blame so that O'Malley would not turn on him and push him out of his job as Taoiseach. The Tribunal was to become politics by another means. Goodman himself was one of the most impressive businessmen I have ever witnessed. I once saw him host a press conference, single handedly, in an upstairs room in the Shelbourne Hotel. He had all the facts at his fingertips and could quote figures and statistics from his business from memory. He had no notes, it was all in his head. He was facing a hostile press but answered every single question and allegation hurled at him in a courteous and calm manner. It was easy to see why he was able to bounce back years later, even though brought to the brink of bankruptcy. Goodman proved to have been a much tougher survivor than Haughey. The drip feed of insinuation and revelation about Haughey had begun. The year ahead was to become an *annus horibilis* for Haughey.

CHAPTER FOURTEEN
GOLDEN CIRCLE

After his humiliating defeat in the Presidential election my father would occasionally ask me to accompany him to events. He felt this terrible isolation. Some of his colleagues in Leinster House were somewhat diffident with him now that he had been thrown unceremoniously into the backbenches. It was not that they were avoiding him but I think quite a few felt embarrassed and to an extent slightly guilty as to what had happened. In the months following the election he was sort of looked upon as a ghost-like reminder of a terrible time. It was like a bereavement scene where people avoid the eyes, and avoid engaging at all. It was to puncture this feeling of isolation we knew he felt, that the family encouraged him to write a book about his experience in the Presidential election.

In any event, after the Presidential, he was to attend the Cairde Fáil event which happens towards Christmas every year. This is an evening dinner event, then held in the Burlington, which mainly draws from supporters, friends and businesspeople who are associated with the party. It is always a good night out and an opportunity to catch up with a lot of people in the one place. This year my father would not be at the top table. He took his own table and invited some constituency people. He wanted me to come along too. Seán Doherty came in on our table. The theme of the evening was Charlie Haughey's 10th year as party leader. There were quite a few well-known people invited to join Haughey at the top table including the actor Richard Harris, the poet Brendan Kennelly, Gay Byrne, Kathleen Watkins, and the singer Chris De Burgh with his wife.

Doherty sat beside me. I knew him a long, long time. When he was being hunted by the press at the height of the phone tapping controversy in 1982 he had stayed in our house. He had actually crashed out in my bedroom because the house was full at the time. My father knew both of the Roscommon deputies, Doherty and Terry Leyden, very well because he had represented the constituency. In fact both of them had been organisation protégées of my father when he was in that constituency. Doherty was normally great company. He is the only person that I met in politics that could send your stomach into muscular spasm because of the laughter he could generate. He had a charming, rogue manner and was, probably because of his training in the Garda Special Branch, a great observer of people. This night, however, he was not in great mood. In fact he was dour. He kept a monologue going all night to me about the iniquities of Haughey and everything he, Haughey, had done over the years. I thought initially he was saying this for my benefit, so that I understood where his sympathies lay in relation to what Haughey had done to my father in the Presidential election. However the dirge continue all night, to the point where it more resembled a bardic poem or curse brought down on Haughey's head. It was clear to me that he had huge issues with Haughey and that he was coming to some form of personal crisis on the matter. Doherty, I emphasise, was not drinking that night, nor in fact at all in that particular period. He kept vowing to me that he would even things up with Haughey and in a way avenge my father along the way. I suggested mildly this was not necessary. Doherty said that was the problem with my father, he was too much of a gentleman. He repeatedly said that politics was a dirty business and that he could show how dirty it could be for Haughey. He referred to Haughey in that quaintly rural term of abuse as a 'tramp'. I kept his conversation to myself and thought nothing more of it.

Haughey, for his part, was revelling in the occasion. It had all the appearance of a feast for a Gaelic Chief. There was a harpist, plucking away at the Irish tunes, while guests ate. Later on it became something of a tribute night given it was his 10th year as leader of the party. The actor Richard Harris made a kind of rambling eulogy, laced with the odd anecdote about Donough O'Malley and the 1960s. Brendan Kennelly, whom I enjoy, composed a poem of outlandish praise for Haughey which probably would have sounded better had it been delivered back in the days of the Gaelic Chiefs' drunken feasts. It was a formal dinner and few were falling around drunk when he delivered his words. Then to round off the evening Chris De Burgh came to the microphone and sang Lady in Red. Despite the big ticket nature of the occasion the response from the audience to Haughey's speech, while enthusiastic, was not as ecstatic as on previous occasions.

The night itself was a complement to Haughey, not just a tribute to him. Haughey had this ability to orchestrate great occasions and make people feel better than themselves and his personality was borne out in the atmosphere of the evening.

Another night, some years previously, my father brought me to what was an event of a more close-in kind. It was hosted in the old Berkeley Court Hotel. P.V. Doyle, the owner of the hotel, was a fan of Haughey and a great friend to my father. The informal dinner would accommodate fifteen to twenty or so people. The guest list was mainly from the world of business and the professions. They all seemed to

share a connection to P.V. Doyle or Haughey. They were
not political types, my father and Haughey were the only
representatives of that profession present. I was thinking of
a career in journalism and to my delight the famous writer
and journalist John Healy was there and I got to talk to him.
He had been a friend of Haughey's since the 1960s and also
had a deep friendship with Douglas Gageby, the legendary
editor of the *Irish Times*. Gageby was the last editor to have
a sympathetic ear to Fianna Fáil.

The discussion was lively and informal. The drink of choice
was Black Velvet, which was poured from largish jugs.
Black Velvet is a mixture of Guinness and Champagne,
mixed together in equal measure. Haughey was relaxed
and appeared to be amongst friends. His friends were
giving it to him and being irreverent. Haughey was able
to take it and would laugh quite a lot through the dinner.
Eventually he had to be carried off or hustled out to the car
and home because he was beginning to topple off his chair.
Somebody joked, "you'd better take him home" to peals of
laughter. The night continued on without him. What struck
me was that he was at ease with people of equivalent status
to him, either in income terms or intelligence. He did not
suffer fools easily. It also brought home to me all of the
claims made over the years, by opponents, that he was in
some sense an intimidating presence. Of course he could
be vulgar and abusive but also gracious and charming.
However Haughey was never a bully to those who stood
up to him or whom he considered his equal. For those who
felt or gave away signals that they could be intimidated,
as sure as night followed day they would be. None of the
people I saw that night grovelled at his feet and for the
most part they ignored him. He was just one of the guests.

But in 1991 the atmosphere was getting less convivial
for Haughey. Apart from the Goodman allegations, it was
to be a year of scandal after scandal. There is not enough

space here to quite capture the depth and detail of these controversies. Suffice it to say that Haughey was not guilty in all of these business or financial transactions but because many of the people at the heart of them were in fact friends, or perceived to be close to him, the media and the public got a bad smell from what was happening. To a great extent people assumed he was involved. As these controversies ranged across the floor of the Dáil and through the media, someone came up with the phrase 'Golden Circle'. It may have been Dick Spring or Pat Rabbitte, both had fairly talented speech writers at the time and were good at capturing the essence of what was happening. The suggestion was that there was a 'Golden Circle' of businesspeople and insiders who were secretly benefiting from public contracts or work. It was a neat phrase and could encompass almost any transaction. The reality, of course, was that with Haughey there would always be a presumption that if there was smoke there was also fire.

The first scandal involved a privatised, state-owned company, the Irish Sugar Company, which upon privatisation became Greencore. Key executives within the company were given a one million pound loan, by the company, to buy shareholdings in a related distribution company. In less than a year, the value of their shares had netted them a profit of over £7 million and all the four executives had to put in was £10,000 each. The controversy was stretched out over a long period, with Bernie Cahill put under the microscope on the matter. Cahill was believed to have been very close to Haughey. He was also Chairman of Aer Lingus and of the Feltrim mining company, in which Haughey's son was a significant shareholder. A separate scandal arose as to whether Haughey had pushed Cahill to accept National City Brokers as the stockbroking advisors to the privatisation of Greencore. Dermot Desmond was the key founder of NCB and known to be a supporter and friend of Haughey. Haughey denied this but it later emerged that Cahill had in fact shown him the shortlist with Cahill denying Haughey brought any influence to bear. Cahill had flown by helicopter from his native Cork to the meeting with Haughey in Kinsealy.

The next controversy concerned the purchase of the old Johnson, Mooney and O'Brien site in Ballsbridge, the most expensive part of Dublin 4. There had been an increase in the price before the property was bought by Eircom for their headquarters. The scandal here impacted on veteran businessman and millionaire Michael Smurfit and again Dermot Desmond was connected to the transaction. In a radio interview, Haughey caused much annoyance to those who were prominent and involved with the transaction when he called on them to "stand aside." Seamus Pairceir, who was involved with one of the companies material to the transaction, but was also Chairman of the Custom House Dockland Authority, a public body, and was one of those asked to stand aside. Pairceir was a distinguished former Head of the Revenue Commissioners. Michael Smurfit was Chairman of Telecom Éireann as it was then known and he was also asked to stand aside. Haughey stated that neither man had done anything wrong but still stated they should stand aside from their positions pending the outcome of the inquiry into the transaction.

Then there was a controversy over how the state advanced money to assist UCD in buying the Carysfort site in Blackrock, Dublin where it's business school is now based. The opposition here centred around meetings that Haughey had with the then UCD President Paddy Masterson, and his apparent deep involvement in encouraging the transaction. The fact that the Carysfort site had been purchased by Pino Harris, another apparent associate of Haughey, and then sold to UCD, was viewed as suspicious.

There were three further controversies that impacted directly on Haughey and his family. Nora Owen of Fine

Gael suggested that a Dublin County Council sewerage pipe that had recently been run through Haughey's Kinsealy property had the convenient effect of improving the value of the property. Some years previous, the Council had reckoned that laying a pipeline across the property was unnecessary but somehow this view had now mysteriously changed. Another controversy was generated by the ESB's decision to install some kind of experimental wind generator in Haughey's island holiday home of Inishvickillane. The controversy centred on the fact that a State Body was supplying free electricity to the sitting Taoiseach. Of course the ESB justified this experiment with wind power on the basis that Inishvickillane was an ideal location for an experiment in wind power.

Ciarán Haughey, the Taoiseach's son, was involved in a helicopter company called Celtic Helicopters. A report on a rival, Aer Lingus-owned company, Irish Helicopters, was apparently sent to Celtic Helicopters by the firm NCB who had been retained to write the report. The report contained confidential material. NCB insisted the report had in fact been posted in error to the wrong company. Because of the Dermot Desmond connection the media and opposition parties presumed the worst.

The detail behind these controversies was not the important issue. As ever, when it comes to parliamentary controversies, it was the response from the relevant authorities that became the story and in effect made the public uneasy about what was going on. For instance, the decision by Haughey to ask Michael Smurfit and Seamus Pairceir to stand aside was illustrative of bad handling on Haughey's part. While denying either man had done anything wrong he nonetheless decided that they should stand aside from their state-appointed positions. It appeased nobody and led to even more suspicion. Haughey, in all of these controversies, through partial or complete denial, had managed to incur even greater suspicion as to what was going on. His whole technique, in responding to questions, seemed to be at odds with the more modern world of 24-hour, around-the-clock news that was then emerging as a phenomenon. As a journalist reporting on these controversies at the time, it seemed to me as if Haughey could do no right. There was a feeding frenzy amongst the journalists chasing these matters. The problem for Haughey was that there were too many sharks in the water and all of them could smell blood. There was an internal rivalry between the opposition leaders at Leinster House. The Labour Leader Dick Spring, by conventional press wisdom, was doing better than the main leader of the opposition John Bruton. Both were trying to outdo each other in terms of harrying Haughey in the Dáil. Haughey was not helping himself. He, at one stage, much to his own disadvantage re-categorised his relationship with Dermot Desmond claiming he was not a friend but merely 'a business friend'. It might have been better if he had said Desmond was someone he knew through business. The description of Desmond as a 'business friend' invited people to ridicule Haughey on the basis of how he categorised friendship. Haughey's sometimes arcane use of language added to his difficulties in this period. It smacked of evasion and people were getting the sense that the semantics were there for a reason.

Some, who were very close to Haughey at this time, suspected the hidden hand of one Albert Reynolds behind many of these controversies. From his position as Minister for Finance, Albert was alleged to have been pulling the levers in the background. The two departments in a government through which a lot of sensitive information passes are the Department of Finance and the office of the Attorney General. There was a suspicion that Albert Reynolds was encouraging these controversies on or leaking material to the media. There was also a new factor in the media scene, where like the competition among party leaders, there was a new operator on the block – the *Sunday Business Post*. Though a business newspaper, its contributors wrote extensively around political matters and even more so where the worlds of politics and business intersected. They were breaking stories in their own right and were at the top of their game under a former *Irish Press* journalist called Damien Kiberd who was very well connected in many different sectors of Irish life.

Over the summer of 1991 discussions got underway on what was called the mid-term review of the policy agreement between the two coalition partners in government. Albert Reynolds and Bertie Ahern were the negotiators on the Fianna Fáil side. Albert Reynolds put the foot down on some of the PDs demands and got credit within Fianna Fáil for getting them to back off in terms of the concessions they were seeking. Speculation of another heave against Haughey began to circulate, with the suggestion being that Reynolds would lead on the challenge. Reynolds, Pádraig Flynn and Ahern were, it was suggested, to go to Haughey, putting it to him that he resign. It appears that Bertie Ahern either got cold feet about the plan or was simply not interested in the approach. Ahern went by himself to Haughey and recommended that he indicate a retirement date. Haughey was agreeable to this suggestion and in front of a meeting of his TDs said he would know when it was time to step down. Haughey pleaded to be allowed to go with dignity. His appeal softened the hearts of deputies. However the group around Reynolds were a ruthless bunch and had unrivalled experience of party infighting. They suspected Haughey was trying the same thing that he had done in 1983 to head off a challenge to his leadership, in other words, buy some time but prepare to fight off the challenge from them.

At this time the Reynolds faction began to suspect that Bertie Ahern was playing a double game; asking Haughey to resign but in actual fact giving him the space and time to make a comeback or recovery. Reynolds named a date for a challenge but seems to have pulled back, fearing, as many contenders for leadership do, that in being the first to move he might succeed in removing Haughey but lose the subsequent leadership vote. Later Reynolds decided to back the motion for a change in the leadership put down by Seán Power TD of Kildare. As his PR Advisor Tom Savage put it, "if he didn't stand up to Haughey now he would never be leader of the party". Reynolds, Pádraig Flynn, Máire Geoghegan-Quinn, and Noel Treacy all staged their announcements that they were supporting the Power motion. They refused to resign from the government, forcing Haughey to sack them. Haughey's credibility as Taoiseach had been taken away by the successive scandals of the previous year, now his authority as head of government and Taoiseach was severely undermined. The wolf pack that was after him was, in the words of the former party fundraiser Des Hanafin, "the same people who had brought down Jack Lynch".

But something of Haughey's appeal to his backbenchers clearly struck a chord. Ahern was popular with TDs and he was very clear in his private re-assurances that Haughey would be moving on. Haughey insisted on an open vote this time. He won 55 to 22. P.J. Mara and others thought this might be the end of it. Some observers were mystified as to why Dad voted support for Haughey but he had always maintained through his career that he would support the incumbent party leader and on principle did not believe in heaves. My father was not too enamoured at the way Reynolds was undermining Haughey. Reynolds said he knew he would lose, so he asked supporters not to declare their hand and wait. Reynolds made a speech claiming his home had been put under surveillance and was being watched by men in a Toyota HiAce van and that vicious rumours were being circulated about him. Most found it hard to believe but it had echoes of similar claims made by O'Malley, Colley and Séamus Brennan during the heaves of an earlier period. Back in 1982 there had been a disgraceful incident in the Dáil car park where supporters of Haughey, who had been drinking in the Dáil bar all day, had attacked and knocked Jim Gibbons to the ground. There were very few Haughey supporters congregating around Leinster House on this occasion. The atmosphere seemed more sombre and less triumphalist than in previous years. Despite Haughey's victory there was still an air uncertainty around his government and his future prospects.

Meanwhile, Albert Reynolds and his colleagues were now free of public office. Albert, for his part, spent most of his time in the Dáil chatting casually to journalists and TD colleagues. He was in no way isolated and appeared to have plenty of friends. Reynolds, who never drank, had endless time and patience for people. He was a consummate listener and had an unerring instinct for understanding what a person wanted from him. Reynolds was driven away from Leinster House, after his failed leadership heave, in a big Jaguar car. He was sending the message, that as a wealthy man in his own right, he had no need for the Ministerial or state-supplied car. Unlike Haughey, Reynolds did not need his job as a minister to support his own lifestyle. It was a potent message he was sending to the public. The departure of Reynolds gave Haughey space to reward two new people with cabinet positions and appoint two others as ministers of state. Disaster befell one of his appointments, Jim McDaid a popular deputy from Donegal who had a successful GP medical practice. Some years previous, McDaid had attended the trial and acquittal of James Pius Clarke, a convicted member of the IRA, who was then facing extradition. The two men had played football together and McDaid gave evidence that he was, in fact, at a stag night with Clarke on the evening when Clarke was alleged to have committed the offences stated by the British authorities on their extradition warrant. Proinsias De Rossa, leader of the Workers Party, raised the matter of a photograph that had been taken of McDaid outside the courthouse. The PDs reacted badly to the controversy and said he was not an appropriate appointment. McDaid met with them and assured them he was no supporter of the IRA. In fact, McDaid was only testifying as would be any citizen's duty if he knew someone to be innocent of the charges being put against them. McDaid went back to Haughey and told him what had transpired. McDaid withdrew his nomination at his own initiative.

The ferocity of the attacks directed against McDaid by Fine Gael and De Rossa meant that the Fianna Fáil backbenches were also in a rage. The fact that the Progressive Democrats had effectively vetoed his appointment, on the premise that he was not suitable or had been compromised, caused even greater annoyance, given that for McDaid not to testify on behalf of Clarke would be the equivalent of perverting the course of justice. The behaviour of the PDs had echoes of their behaviour during the Presidential election in relation to my father. Nerves were still raw in Fianna Fáil. However the McDaid case was, arguably, far worse than that of my father as it represented a gross injustice to McDaid and his reputation. Haughey appeared passive, almost compliant, in his approach to the whole matter. Rather than deal with the matter himself he sent McDaid off to discuss the nomination, with his own accusers in the PDs. Haughey was no longer exercising any real leadership in the government, he was simply outsourcing decisions, on his own nomination, to his coalition partners. The idea that the PDs were now effectively running Haughey was too much for most Fianna Fáil deputies to stomach. There were already TDs demanding that the parliamentary party should meet.

Seán Doherty then came into the picture. He gave an interview to a light entertainment programme on RTÉ called *Nighthawks*. It was hosted by Shay Healy, who was not part of the RTÉ current affairs team. The interview was recorded from a pub in Roscommon called Hell's Kitchen. The interview was well flagged in advance, with the RTÉ News stating that Healy would again be raising the issue of the tapping of two journalists' phones. Doherty had previously told *Magill* magazine some years before that he was tired of 'carrying the can' for the phone tapping incident. The interview on television hinted the same again and indicated that others may have known about the tapping. Pádraig Flynn subsequently said on radio that Doherty should have been more specific. Seán Doherty did not let him down. Doherty hosted a press conference that ran right up against the 9pm television News deadline. Most of his press conference ran live and unedited because there was an RTÉ camera workers strike on at the time. This unedited footage lent even more credibility to what he was saying. Doherty said bluntly that he had handed the transcripts of the tapped telephone calls directly to Haughey, something the latter denied and continued to try to do again in the days ahead.

Des O'Malley describes what happened next:

"The last straw came when Seán Doherty confirmed what we always suspected was the truth behind the telephone-tapping in 1982. The revelation during a television interview that Haughey was centrally involved brought the end within sight. I've no doubt the Doherty intervention was orchestrated. I went to see Haughey, and our conversation was brief and to the point. I said "This can't go on." He told me he'd think about the situation; but he was realistic enough to recognise reality. There was no real fight from him this time. He knew he couldn't carry a majority in the

> *Fianna Fáil parliamentary party. If he somehow had attempted to carry on he would have been removed as leader by his own colleagues.'*[67]

There are of course other versions of why Haughey had to go in the end. There are a number of conspiracy theories surrounding the Seán Doherty intervention. One of these stories suggests that Doherty got handsomely paid by a senior businessman or number of businessmen to take Haughey out. Veronica Guerin, the investigative journalist, who had previously worked with Haughey on the Forum for a New Ireland, was convinced about this particular theory and spoke to me about it afterwards. Veronica had a great nose for a story but even she, with all her contacts, was unable to stand this particular story up. My own view is a simple one. Doherty was annoyed at Haughey and took matters into his own hands. I think he did co-ordinate what he did with others involved in the Albert Reynolds campaign. Doherty had become quite religious and was looking for some kind of apotheosis in his life. He knew his career and reputation would be forever stained by this one event in 1982 unless he did something to offset it. The decision to come clean on the whole matter was his way of doing this. He always insisted that the placing of the wiretaps was justified in terms of the cabinet's concerns about leaks from its discussions. Cabinet confidentiality is considered an important dimension to the work of a government. Whether breaches to the principle of Cabinet confidentiality are a singular threat to the security of the state is a point of debate.

Catherine Butler, Haughey's Personal Assistant, has spoken, during the *Haughey* documentary series by Mint Productions, of how Dr John O'Connell had come to the Taoiseach before the Seán Doherty event and insisted that he should stand down for both health and political

[67]O'Malley, Desmond, *Conduct Unbecoming – A Memoir*, Gill & Macmillan, 2014, p. 189

reasons. O'Connell had a strong influence and friendship with Haughey down the years. He had been the conduit of a donation payment to Haughey from an Arab gentleman who had an interest in acquiring an Irish passport. At that time there was a scheme whereby an investor in an Irish company could acquire an Irish passport. The payment to Haughey was allegedly for a horse but the Tribunal of Inquiry appeared skeptical on this point. After the McDaid appointment fiasco my father and O'Connell, it was informally agreed, would tell Haughey when it was the right time to stand down. Haughey had apparently agreed to this. Unfortunately, despite the goodwill involved in this approach, events overtook the arrangement. At that point in time there was such a chasm of disbelief between Haughey and members of his own party that few actually believed he would retire voluntarily, even if he were to give categorical assurances on that point. His form, as opposed to his pedigree, in racing parlance did not lend itself to believing that he would honour such an arrangement.

The formal Haughey valedictory speech to the Dáil was noted for its reference to Shakespeare and a quote from the play *Othello*: "I have done the state some service; they know't: No more of that". His final year and months in office had all of the elements of drama that one associates with a Shakespearean tragedy. Few knew at the point of his retirement that in fact his quieter days would be ruptured by revelations about his personal finances. Haughey's retirement from politics was going to prove as stormy as his long years in office.

CHAPTER FIFTEEN
LEGACY

In 1996 rumours began to circulate about a large donation of over a million pounds that was given to a prominent former politician. The stories began to sweep the country. Journalists began a frenzied effort to see if the person receiving this money could be named. The dogs on the street knew it had to involve Haughey. The dam holding back the tide of revelations burst when Fine Gael minister Michael Lowry was forced to resign from the John Bruton-led coalition because of a business arrangement he had with the supermarket retailer Ben Dunne. Dunne was in dispute with his family and the matter had gone to law. With the lawyers involved, the circle of knowledge about this one million plus payment to Haughey began to widen. It was not long before the media, still unable to name Haughey, were writing of the details of the payment but not naming the parties involved. Haughey was referred to constantly in the press as 'Mr You Know Who'. At the time I had been nominated by Bertie Ahern to run for the Dáil in the forthcoming election. As soon as I was nominated I had a team out doing door-to-door walkabouts in the constituency so that I could be introduced early to the electorate. I was contesting the five seat Dublin South

West constituency which incorporated areas like Tallaght, Clondalkin, Greenhills and Newcastle, County Dublin.

One evening we were doing a walkabout in Kingswood Heights, a middle class enclave in Tallaght that lies between the Red Cow Roundabout and the Belgard Road. Things were going well and as yet the issue of Haughey, our former leader, had not been raised by any of the constituents. Towards nine o'clock in the evening we stopped our efforts and headed for the local public house, the Clock Tower. The drinks were ordered and the team and I fell to discussing how we would deal with the Haughey issue on the doorsteps, if and when things came out and if the subject was, as expected, an immense controversy. The usual scenarios were thrown around the company; distance ourselves, emphasise the local as distinct to the national, denounce him altogether. In the midst of these musings a friend from Belfast piped in, "You know when all is said and done Haughey will probably be remembered as being good for the country but bad for politics". It was, to my mind, a very accurate summation of the Haughey career. Another activist shrewdly said, rather than address the detail of what Haughey did, we should use this line as a way of closing off the issue if it came up on the doorsteps. Months later I was at the Royal Hibernian Academy, where a bust of the journalist John Healy, an inveterate Haughey friend, was being donated. It was a large banquet and I was seated in the company of some members of the Gallagher, property developer family. They asked how was the Haughey thing going down with the voters and how did we handle it. I told them the yarn about how we came up with the line from the Belfast man's comments. They fell around the place laughing at the cleverness of it all. It had then, of course, emerged that he had received bank drafts to the value of £1.3 million from Ben Dunne. Haughey put in his usual flat denial but later had to admit he had received the money and in effect apologise to his own legal team whom he had also misled on this matter.

"The Moriarty tribunal was then established to investigate payments received by Haughey and by Lowry. The tribunals possessed legal powers to secure disclosure of records and command testimony unavailable to previous inquirers, and their hearings revealed to an eager public that Haughey's lifestyle had rested on payment from some of the country's richest men, sometimes disguised as political donations, and supplemented from such dubious sources as the fund raised to pay for Brian Lenihan's liver operation."[68]

A few years later in 2004, I was now a member of the Dáil that has set up the Moriarty Tribunal. I went up to meet Bertie Ahern for lunch in Malahide. I was there to discuss issues around his appointment of me as Editor of *The Nation*, a party magazine. When finished the lunch I put in a call to Haughey. He answered himself and I asked was he okay for a visit. Arriving at Kinsealy it was immediately apparent that times had changed. The wooden security hut in the long driveway that led up to the gates, in years past occupied by a Garda, was now clearly empty and abandoned. In her interview with the Mint Productions documentary on Haughey, his daughter Eimear described his position at this time as virtually being 'under house arrest'.

Haughey took me into his study. We had a brief discussion about Meda Ryan's new book that covered Tom Barry and the War of Independence period. He had read the book and enjoyed it. Haughey was always well read. I mentioned casually that I was now Editor of *The Nation* and if he wanted to do an interview it would be good to do one. He pulled a letter from his desk. He said he would be delighted to do an interview but added "look at this letter from my lawyer". <u>The letter w</u>arned him against engaging in any public

[68]Maume, Patrick, *Monograph for the Royal Irish Academy*, Dictionary of Irish Biography

interviews of any kind and enclosed a communication that the lawyer had received from the Moriarty Tribunal. The tribunal was making the point that, while Mr Haughey's lawyers were advancing medical reasons as to why their client would not be up to the pressure of testifying before it, he was doing television interviews. Haughey had just participated as an interviewee in a documentary about the arts scene in the 1960s. Haughey was adamant that "I better not do anymore".

At that point I said to him that I thought he should see if he could find a biographer or documentary maker, who was favourably disposed, and would get to work on his life story. I said that if this was not done, while he was still reasonably well, then the story on his life would be wholly and utterly dominated by the current tribunal inquiry. It was, I said, a matter of his personal and historical legacy. He became quite curious and mentioned the names of journalists and writers who had already broached the subject matter with him. He was seeking advice on whom to trust. We had a wider discussion about biographers where I warned him that some of these get very tired, while doing the painstaking research, and in effect turn against the subject of the biography. I said it would be safer if he and the family started with getting a documentary series made where he would nominate friends to co-operate as interviewees. He thought this was a good idea and I think it was this that led to the Mint Productions series on Haughey. Our conversation then turned to current politics. He was critical of all of the money that Bertie and the government were spending. I did not mention to him that I had just met Bertie in Malahide. On previous occasions Haughey had been critical of him. This time he was a little bit more gracious about Ahern than he had been on previous occasions. It clearly rankled somewhat with Haughey that Bertie Ahern, whom he saw as something of a protégée, had escalated his difficulties by establishing the Moriarty Tribunal.

The source of Haughey's apparent fortune was an issue from the day he began in public life. It featured in the 1960s, the 1970s, the 1980s and again, to his ultimate cost in the 1990s. The laws of libel, cautious or deferential journalism, and fear on the part of the banks lending him the money to support his lifestyle, were the main reasons why little if nothing emerged on this front while he was actively engaged in public life. Des O'Malley surmised that much of his money must have come from property development and his friendship with the Gallagher construction empire:

"We guessed that he had benefactors whose welfare was bound up with his own. For example, how had he made his money in the first place? After all, he did not come from a moneyed background. In the 1950s he was a partner in a small accountancy practice in Amiens Street, Dublin at a time when no-one had a bob and Amiens Street was no better an address than it is now. Yet out of this he was able to buy Grangemore, a country house in is own grounds beyond Raheny. When he sold that for development he was able to trade up to Kinsealy."[69]

Patrick Gallagher had been very open over the years about his and his father's sponsorship of Haughey. They, he told me on many occasions, suggested to Haughey that he buy Grangemore, a Victorian pile on 45-acres, and then proceeded to buy it off him for the then huge sum of £200,000. Gallagher laughed off the transaction, in the Mint Productions documentary, stating that this particular deal was even better for the Gallaghers than it was for Haughey. So, it is clear Haughey's first fortune came because of the foresight of the Gallaghers in spotting a property that would eventually be changed for housing and tipping their friend off to buy it so that they could then, later, buy it off him. This sale clearly allowed Haughey to live way beyond

[69]O'Malley, Desmond, *Conduct Unbecoming – A Memoir*, Gill & Macmillan, 2014, p. 125

his paltry ministerial and TD income right up to the 1970s. Presumably, when he lost his ministerial job as a result of the Arms Trial, his income went down but his outgoings went up. He was travelling the country, clawing his way back to a position of power, and to outward appearances there had been no change in his financial circumstances. When Haughey became Taoiseach in 1979 a huge overdraft had built up, in excess of a million pounds. Patrick Gallagher stepped in again and helped to reduce the indebtedness, with security being taken against Haughey's newest and most valuable asset, Abbeville in Kinsealy. This turned out to be a figment and not enforceable in law. This allowed Haughey to borrow against the property in the future if he needed to. His work done for Haughey, Patrick Gallagher then went bankrupt in his own business and was no longer in a position to continue the family role of long-term support to Haughey.

The settlement with AIB in 1979, with Gallagher's assistance, allowed Haughey to go on again with his high maintenance lifestyle, and that appears to have lasted until he was again under pressure from the bank, this time around when he became Taoiseach again in 1987 and for his final period as Taoiseach. On this occasion Ben Dunne stepped in to finance his difficulties, with Haughey using the now immortal words, on receipt of the donated bank drafts, "thanks a million, big fella". One of the mistakes Haughey appears to have made in his dealings with this money from Dunne was to allow his fear of public disclosure to prevail.

When Dunne's sister sent their solicitor, Noel Smith, up to Kinsealy to sort the whole matter out, Haughey was in denial, even about the fact that they money had actually been given.

When Haughey's 1987 government turned out to be a success and the economy recovered he was, as Taoiseach, to acquire a new set of benefactors and donors including the likes of Dermot Desmond, who has made it clear, in the tribunal and in interviews, that he would have been delighted to support Haughey now and again because of what he had done with the Irish Financial Services Centre. The Tribunal of Inquiry concluded that Haughey had given a material benefit to Ben Dunne, by dint of his intervention with the Revenue Commissioners on behalf of the Dunnes and their large tax liability. It is hard not to conclude, on the basis of the tribunal evidence, and the consistent sponsorship of Haughey by various businessmen that, in effect, he spent the most part of his political life from the 1960s onwards either in debt to the bank or as a 'kept man' of an elite group of business friends.

The lengths to which Haughey went to hide the money he was receiving was a real source of shock to the public. The elaborate scheme put in place by his accountant and friend Des Traynor, involving off-shore accounts in the Cayman islands, did incalculable damage to Haughey, but even more impactfully, to the entire political system.

It was left, ironically, to his early protégée, Bertie Ahern as Taoiseach to tidy up in the wake of the revelations about Haughey. There followed a series of controls and regulation placed upon those elected to Leinster House. Spending limits were imposed on what parties could actually spend at election times. Separately, there were disclosure limits, above which all donations had to be recorded and reported to a new Standards in Public Office Commission. Ministerial office holders and members of the Oireachtas were now to be required to declare all sources of income they received on an official register, with rigorous investigation by the new Commission if breaches of ethics legislation were either breached or reported to have been evaded. The Irish political class were the subject of an intense series of measures that represented a regulatory clean up that many might have felt should have been done a long time previous to this.

Under this current system it would be virtually impossible for someone like Haughey to emerge again. This does not, of course, mean that wealthy, interested persons, will not be able to find a way to attempt to manipulate the political system as they do both in Ireland and elsewhere.

Any assessment of Haughey cannot ignore the extraordinary and prodigious policies and legislative achievements he managed to log in the 1960s. This was, in Haughey terms, his golden era. He was a progressive politician, making the most of an economic rise to widen the net of social provision. His measures were both enlightened and in the long run to prove costly. Free travel for the elderly did not come cheap but is one of the few social welfare type benefits that has proven so far irreversible. The enlightened approach he took towards the arts and the position of the artist in society was genuinely novel. The tax break on royalty income sent a signal, but his creation of the Aosdána scheme, a similar structure to the Académie française, was a practical help to working artists. Haughey's life-long friendship with the poet and writer Anthony Cronin, who was appointed his cultural advisor, is testimony to his commitment in this area. Apart from the arts-related buildings that he secured funding for, Haughey was prepared to give his moral patronage to those engaged in the arts. His moral patronage and support meant a great deal more, given the important positions he held in government. It is fair to say that before Haughey's arrival, the arts scene was an impoverished constituency, on the margins of society, but certainly not viewed as being part of the mainstream of Irish life.

Those who worked as public servants in the national, or cultural, institutions of state were always guaranteed a ready ear with Haughey. His appointments to public positions often reflected this. George Eogan, the country's foremost archaeologist, was appointed as a Taoiseach's nominee to the Upper House or Senate. Eogan was the archaeologist who began the dig at Knowth and Dowth in

Co Meath that was to become such a treasure in terms of a window on Irish antiquity.

If Haughey's career had stopped in the 1960s there would still have been a lot to write about, though not enough to fill the countless numbers of books that exist. It is fair to assert that the political or historical period from the 1960s to the 1990s is in effect worthy of being called the Haughey era. Other political figures came and went during this period but Haughey was and remains the one constant. He was also, interestingly, the one political figure, against whom or for, people responded to. There were, in truth, very few people who were neutral about Charlie Haughey. Even his friend and schoolmate George Colley became a relative obsessive about his influence and the danger he presented to the Fianna Fáil party. In May 1967 he, Colley, flagged his concerns to a Fianna Fáil Youth Conference in Galway asking the young people gathered there not to be 'dispirited if some people in high places appear to have low standards'. This was a siren call to battle by Colley in what was to be lifelong struggle against Haughey. Colley was a poster boy for the more traditional and conservative elements within Fianna Fáil, the very people that Seán Lemass was gently trying to move on. It was left to younger men, like Haughey and my father, not just to move them on but take these older gentlemen out of their Dáil seats.

There was both a brashness and optimism to the 1960s. Haughey ran up against the older generation, or 'old guard', as they were called in Fianna Fáil. This earlier generation was imbued with the asceticism of the early Sinn Féin philosophy. Haughey's ambition and wealth were, in many ways, an affront for everything they had lived in their meager but successful lives. There was a generational as well as a social snobbery that Haughey was to invoke amongst some in the party. He was not from one of the party's well established blood-lines and was seen therefore as a parvenu. Some of the older types also distrusted him because his father had been a ' Free State' man or followed the legacy of Michael Collins.

The main rupture in Haughey's career was the Arms Trial. People have tried to apply all sorts of motives and *mala fides* to his actions at this time. In truth, my father always felt him to be a victim of this crisis, rather than its author. The raw reality was that Haughey was caught off side, in what was a legitimate operation of state, which went badly wrong. It would have been a clear breach of international law for the Irish state to provide weapons directly to nationalists in the north and encourage an insurgency. Hence the secrecy and surreptitious nature of how the government went about its business in this area. Responsibility for the operation was given to Military Intelligence and the Department of Finance with a discreet, cabinet sub-committee, to co-ordinate the activity in its own right. There was no real need for meetings since there was, in effect, no real requirement for it to report back to the cabinet. Its membership and the key players were all in the cabinet. The key players on the military intelligence side were regular visitors to ministers, government buildings and the relevant decision makers. Haughey's job in the covert operation of state was to facilitate the activity with Department of Finance funding. This he did diligently and to the letter. The truth, which has never really been made explicit over the years, is that the arms importation was fully sanctioned, fully known about and part of a covert action exercise by the state. It had to have plausible deniability built into its mandate and a certain looseness around the definitions around what the relief of distress in the north allowed the people involved to do. The head of government Jack Lynch was fully aware of what was going on and the evidence of this is not just confined to admissions made to me by my father but is confirmed by a variety of different sources and accounts. When the arms importation operation itself started to go wrong, those who had it in for

Haughey and Blaney anyway seized their opportunity to do away with them, foolishly though, pushing the matter too far by putting them on trial. Even Jack Lynch's supporters find it hard to understand his lapses of memory and frankly flawed recollection of what he knew and when around this particular Arms Crisis. The plain fact is that he was running away from his own personal knowledge of the matter.

The Arms Trial was both the undoing of Haughey, then in his early career, but it was also the making of him. When he peered over the wreckage of his own career at that point he had the allegiance and power base of the more republican wing of Fianna Fáil. The fact that Blaney and Boland left the party meant he was now the champion of the republication element within the party. This section of the party, who like him remained on in the party, were a significant source of support and propelled him back into key positions within the party structure within a short number of years. However, the whole crisis had the effect of making him very cautious, perhaps more so than he had been beforehand. His horse riding accident where he fractured his skull, on the eve of the budget, seems to have shaken him. Others maintained this was the case, including the journalist Raymond Smith, and also my father. It is, all the same, a speculative reason for much of the indecision that was to plague him in later years. Such was the fervor of his republican support within the party they were prepared to overlook his other issues and indiscretions whether these were financial or sexual.

Opinions vary about Haughey's leadership style. In times of uncertainty about his own position, he could be prone to tantrums and also bad judgment. There were also suggestions that he tried to micro manage individual departments too much. However Albert Reynolds struck a very different note in his autobiography when he said:

"I had always found Haughey a very fair leader. As a minister, if you did your job well, he did not interfere

but only encouraged. True, he always wanted the job done yesterday and was a stickler for time - but he lived by the same rules himself. He was also strict and though he was always ready to praise good work, any raw recruit caught not performing would be eaten alive!"[70]

One of Haughey's biggest failures when he did eventually become Taoiseach was his handling of the north as an issue. His initial decision to embrace Mrs Thatcher was a good one but his decision to spite her over the Falklands was a poor judgment call. My father viewed his attitude on the British effort to claim back the islands as heedless. It only antagonised Thatcher and meant his successor as Taoiseach, Garret FitzGerald, was then in a position to build a more formal agreement off the back of his ground-breaking summit with Thatcher at Dublin Castle.

My father was on instructions to hype the potential from the Dublin Castle Summit but felt it was the wrong thing to do at the time. Likewise he felt Haughey's opposition to the Anglo-Irish Agreement doubly stupid. My father made it a condition of his becoming Foreign Minister that he be allowed independence in operating this agreement and winning further concessions from the British regarding fair employment for Catholics in the north. Part of Haughey's frustration with Thatcher was clearly to do with the hunger strikes that handed a victory to the IRA and ironically precipitated the Adams and McGuinness wing of Sinn Féin towards a more political path. Haughey's response to the H-Block hunger strike was far more conservative than perhaps his republican backwoodsmen would have liked.

His climb back from the setback of the Arms Trial and his period in the wilderness have been written about extensively. It connected him back to the Fianna Fáil supporter base and allowed him to recruit his own people in the organisation. The landslide election result for

[70]Reynolds, Albert, *My Autobiography*, Transworld Ireland, 2009

Fianna Fáil in 1977 saw a lot of his people elected to the Dáil. This largely went unnoticed, at the time, given the extraordinary popularity of Jack Lynch. The campaign to destabilise Lynch has been greatly exaggerated. In fact Lynch was due to retire anyhow. Lynch and the faction around him had become seriously out of touch with public opinion and the feelings of the parliamentary party. Lynch and the group around him, who emerged in the wake of the Arms Trial, were as complacent and traditional as the Old Guard who were in effect their sponsors. They paid very little heed to the backbenches and were surprised when they revolted in the manner that they did. Haughey's main failing in his wilderness years was that he failed to outline a comprehensive vision of how the country would operate under his rule. He was so cautious in his approach that he steered clear of outlining hard policies both on the North and on the economy. Perhaps he was too afraid of losing support or creating hostages to fortune. He may have been correct in relation to the north but on the economy it might have helped him in 1981. His main opportunity was to be a kinder or less vociferous version of Mrs Thatcher, adapted for local circumstances.

His initial embrace of 'fiscal rectitude' with his 1980 address to the nation was his best intervention since coming to power. His failure to follow through and the speed with which he jettisoned the concept can only be put down to electoral jitters or plain old indecisiveness. In effect this failure of nerve gave a weapon to both his internal critics and those like FitzGerald who wanted strong medicine for the economy. If he had taken the harsh measures in his first administration he would have been in a perfect position as the FitzGerald government faltered and then collapsed over the budget of 1982. His internal critics had two sticks to beat him with, the old Arms Trial issue and the newer one of indecision on the economy. People said of him then that he appeared to be better when his back was up against a wall rather than if he were leading from the front. His image of ruthlessness was entirely belied by the softness with which he dealt with Colley and others who were openly challenging his leadership. His decision to expel O'Malley and crackdown on the dissidents came too late in the day. When he did expel O'Malley from Fianna Fáil he was creating an instant opening for O'Malley to start his own party. The Progressive Democrats denied him a majority in 1987, arguably his best opportunity ever to win the elusive majority. It seems Haughey, together with most of the established parties, had missed the opportunity to create an issue around public anger over high rates of taxes. O'Malley saw the gap on taxation and championed it through his party and on into government.

Haughey's 1987 to 1989 government can, rightly, claim to be the government that led the Irish economic recovery and to have put down the building blocks for the subsequent Celtic Tiger. He can also claim to have initiated the first, albeit modest, contacts with Sinn Féin and the IRA that became the peace process under Albert Reynolds and Bertie Ahern. Reynolds, very wisely, decided to re-appoint Martin Mansergh. Mansergh, the son of an Anglo-Irish historian, became a key advisor to Haughey on the north having previously worked in the Department of Foreign Affairs. Haughey had a good eye for good advisors. Apart from Mansergh there were a great many others he hired over the years who were to serve him well; David Cabot, on environmental issues, Lord Killanin on heritage issues, Anthony Cronin on culture, and of course P.J. Mara on communications.

Though Haughey has given his name to an era in Irish public life it is surprising, and to an extent over looked, that he only managed to achieve one sustained period of four years in office as Taoiseach. He very nearly ruined this by calling an election in 1989. The other periods in office were blighted by instability. In 1979 he had taken over from a wildly popular Taoiseach that gave him a little over a year and a half until there was an election. His nine-month long administration in 1982 was to be the most accident-prone government in living history. His final year in office was blighted by a rash of business scandals that had a side impact on him, bringing to a conclusion his hold on power.

The enigma of Haughey and the Haughey era is that it managed to last so long despite so many, repeated, warnings of the potential danger it could pose. Haughey's triumph is one of survival and success. The successes were mainly in the 1960s and again on his final run in power. In a way, Haughey failed because he was not able to define himself in a different way to his Fianna Fáil predecessors. Jack Lynch was his enemy and rode a wave of personality-based populism that was unique, and different to either Lemass or de Valera. When Haughey got his turn the age of populist politics was running out of road. Politics was becoming more defined around concepts of rational consumer choice, in other words, what are you going to do for me? Haughey could well have framed a persuasive philosophy of his own but failed to do so. He preferred to borrow from both Lemass and de Valera. He became a hybrid of both without the benefits that both men had previously brought to the table of populist politics. Haughey did do his successors in Fianna Fáil a favour by being the first to actually form a coalition. He got no thanks for this.

While Haughey was a great fan of Seán Lemass he did not share the same, diffident, low profile or business-like approach to politics. In any event, Haughey's decision to have a significant lifestyle in the 1960s made it impossible for him to copy the modest, ascetic, approach of his predecessors. His leadership cult did share some of the remoteness of de Valera. The Arms Trial 'debacle' as Haughey called it did afford him an opportunity to re-invent himself as a business prophet of increased independence and a freer, more open, republic.

Haughey, in all of his struggles to get back on top of the pile, neglected to look beyond mere populist politics. He made grandiloquent speeches that hinted at vision but were never in fact fully followed through. The extent to which he failed to follow through with a personal vision is thrown into sharp relief when he is compared to his rival in office Dr Garret FitzGerald. While ultimately FitzGerald failed, he came within five seats of toppling the monopoly dominance of Fianna Fáil over the political and administrative system. FitzGerald may not have thought out the consequences of his secular crusade for a 'pluralist Ireland'. However, the fact that he had a personal vision propelled him into the public consciousness. The Haughey-FitzGerald conflict was the last great intellectual debate in Irish politics. FitzGerald spelled out his vision while Haughey found it safer simply to define himself as being against it. Haughey's opposition to the secular project did not have within it an alternative as to how Ireland would be modernised. He therefore became a disappointment to both conservative and liberal supporters. Haughey himself was a moderniser, in his early career, but seems to have failed to articulate his plans for the future. His opposition to divorce was utterly tactical, and in a sense destructive in its instinct. He was psychologically and otherwise unsuited to pushing Ireland down a more theocratic or traditional route.

"Haughey was essentially a technician of power rather than an ideologue and his inconsistencies must be seen in that light."[71]

On a purely personal level he was not anything like the menace his life-long critics claimed he was. He was not nor never became a direct threat to Irish democracy. In fact it is a testament to the robustness of Irish democracy that it was able to contain Haughey.

---

[71]Maume, Patrick, Monograph for Royal Irish Academy, *Dictionary of Irish Biography*

Over the years Haughey was often accused of adopting a bullying approach to those whom he worked with. My own aunt, Mary O'Rourke, takes the view that this was only the case with people who felt intimidated by him. In her own case she was offered a front bench position by Haughey in relation to women's issues. She was not so keen on being pidgeon-holed on gender issues. She told him so when he called. He seemed a little taken aback by this approach but promised to ring her back. Mary's husband took the view that she would not be offered anything else. Haughey rang her back and offered the better portfolio of Education, one for which, given her profession as teacher, she was much better qualified for, thus showing that in fact those who engaged with him as equals won his attentive respect.

Haughey was rarely, if ever rude, on an interpersonal basis. He struck me as someone who was direct, analytical and very reflective. His upbringing, in straightened circumstances, left him with a determination to enjoy the finer things of life. Behind the outward appearances of wealth and opulence was a man totally insecure and vulnerable when it came to money. Most of his political life was spent trying to keep up with the bills and keep the banks and creditors at bay. He preferred to spend his way out of trouble both in the personal sense and in the public sense. His greatest period as Taoiseach was when the country and he had their backs to the wall. He had no choice but to pare back on spending. He was not a frozen figure, devoid of all emotion. He broke down in tears on several occasions, once when under a barrage of internal pressure at the New Ireland Forum and again when his personal assistant told him that my father was at death's door and would need a liver transplant. When he came across people looking for money or assistance, even on walkabouts, he would slip his hand into his jacket pocket and produced a £20 note. He could be generous and certainly was not, in any sense, tight fisted.

"In a society where limited imagination and ignorance of its own colonised mentality had prevented an

organic development from tradition to modernity, Charles Haughey was the inevitable product of his times. He lived and ruled through an era when old values were being dissolved and turned into money. Bereft of a personal vision, he tried to stimulate the impression of a visionary based on parodying ancient values and their adherents, even while he was up to his oxters in the green slime of the material world. He used the money he got from merchant princes to create the illusion of magic."[72]

In some respects Haughey was good for the country but in others terribly damaging to the practice and conduct of politics. The revelations about his lifestyle induced huge cynicism about the political system in Ireland. It is impossible to convince a young generation that the practice of politics is a noble pursuit. There is an underlying problem in all of this for the country itself. The pervasive cynicism about Irish politics gives support to more, seemingly, radical forces in the society who are bereft of the political skills to make it actually happen. Haughey, with all of his flaws, was on occasion able to make big things happen. Perhaps the last word should be left to the former Fine Gael Taoiseach Liam Cograve, who recognised this, when stating "he achieved more than his critics".

---

[72]Waters, John, *Was it for This? Why Ireland lost the Plot*, By John Waters, Transworld Publishers, 2012

Appendix I

Oifig an Taoisigh
Office of the Taoiseach

31 October 1990

Mr Brian Lenihan, T.D.,
Tánaiste and Minister for Defence.

A Thánaiste, a Aire,

I am writing to request you, pursuant to Article 28.9.4° of the
Constitution, for reasons which I deem to be sufficient, to
resign as a member of the Government.

I should like you to know that, in the event of failure to comply
with this request, I shall with great regret be compelled to
advise the President to terminate your appointment as a member of
the Government.

Yours sincerely,

Taoiseach

Oifig an Taoisigh. Tithe an Rialtais Baile Átha Cliath 2.
Office of the Taoiseach. Government Buildings Dublin 2.

218